ιg purity of this show will ͜ lament of its confused and damaged youngsters speaks directly to us. In its refined, imaginative simplicity, it daringly reverses all the conventional rules by returning the American musical to an original state of innocence. *Spring Awakening* is the best new musical I've seen in a generation."

—JOHN HEILPERN, *NEW YORK OBSERVER*

"An unexpected jolt of sudden genius! A groundbreaking must-see musical sure to wake up Broadway! Edgy in its brutally honest, unromanticized depiction of human sexuality, the night is made heart-rending and magical by themes common to all."

—CLIVE BARNES, *NEW YORK POST*

"Fantastic! Sheer exuberance exploding in a burst of power pop. The new indie-rock treatment of Frank Wedekind's play about hormonal adolescents has just about everything going for it. Be prepared to say, 'Oh, I didn't know musicals could do *that*.'"

—JEREMY MCCARTER, *NEW YORK MAGAZINE*

"Tearing into the pretend pop and reused plots that pass for new musicals on Broadway today, this primal scream of turbulent puberty is furious, serious fun."

—LINDA WINER, *NEWSDAY*

"The most explosive new musical since *Rent*. A gorgeous score. A passionate story. *Spring Awakening* is a remarkable musical that every generation is likely to appreciate now and in years to come."

—MICHAEL SOMMERS, *STAR-LEDGER* (NEWARK)

"*Spring Awakening*, with book and lyrics by Steven Sater and superb indie-rock anthems by Duncan Sheik, throbs with dark humor and dangerous desire. The music, alternately brattish punk and yearning power ballads, reaches the heart of Wedekind's tormented adolescents. *Spring Awakening* is a cult hit in the making if ever I saw one."

—CHARLES SPENCER, *TELEGRAPH* (LONDON)

"The most thrilling pop musical ever. Veteran pop composer Duncan Sheik and lyricist/book writer Steven Sater capture the melancholy and mortification of adolescence with all of the intensity it deserves and none of the condescension it so often receives."

—ERIC GRODE, *NEW YORK SUN*

"I saw *Spring Awakening* exactly thirty-eight days ago, and I haven't gone a day without replaying it in my head since. Two sensuous ballads, 'Touch Me' and 'The Word of Your Body,' are so gorgeous, they already rank among the best ever written for the stage. The main love story is nothing short of Greek tragedy. *Spring Awakening* is an intoxicating experience."

—JOHN MOORE, *DENVER POST*

"Exhilarating. A show that bristles with rawness, vitality and urgency. Sater's book and lyrics seem to capture from within the uniquely teenage feeling that every emotion is the most tempestuous, frightening, passionate or exciting one ever experienced."

—DAVID ROONEY, *VARIETY*

"*Spring Awakening* is a breathtaking dissection of what it means to grow up. In its exploration of new-found sexuality—when everything is extreme, with never a shade of gray—the show rips through the Eugene O'Neill Theatre with pounding intensity. When it is at its alternative-rock best, it sweeps the audience into its beat; when it is at its most poignant, you feel like the only person in the theater."

—HOWARD SHAPIRO, *PHILADELPHIA INQUIRER*

"*Spring Awakening* is an extraordinary new musical. Melodies like 'The Song of Purple Summer' reach deep inside the listener and stir feelings that may have been sleeping for a long time. It's what great theater should do. It's what *Spring Awakening* does."

—RICHARD OUZOUNIAN, *TORONTO STAR*

"Breathtaking. Sheik's iridescent music and Sater's imagistic lyrics make everyone recall when they, too, were young, unshakably set on radicalizing the world. It's electrifying."

—LEONARD JACOBS, *BACKSTAGE*

SPRING AWAKENING
A MUSICAL

BOOK AND LYRICS BY
STEVEN SATER

MUSIC BY
DUNCAN SHEIK

NICK HERN BOOKS
London
www.nickhernbooks.co.uk

A Nick Hern Book

Spring Awakening: A Musical first published in Great Britain in 2021 as a paperback original by Nick Hern Books Limited, The Glasshouse, 49a Goldhawk Road, London W12 8QP, by special arrangement with Theatre Communications Group, Inc., New York

Cover image of the 2021 Almeida Theatre cast: photograph by Alessio Bolzoni; concept by Émilie Chen
Designed and typeset by Lisa Govan for Theatre Communications Group, Inc.
Printed in the UK by Mimeo Ltd, Huntingdon, Cambridgeshire PE29 6XX

A CIP catalogue record for this book is available from the British Library

ISBN 978 1 83904 044 3

For my parents; and my children;
and for you, L...

—S.S.

PREFACE

> When we were young Frank Wedekind was the
> Masked Man of our *Spring Awakening*... This was the
> turn of the century. Bourgeois ideas lay in their
> agony.
>
> —BERTHOLD VIERTEL (1885–1953),
> *WRITINGS ON THEATRE*

Suffice it to say, by the time I thought of introducing Wedekind's Masked Man to the American musical theater, those same "bourgeois ideas" had more than managed to rise again.

It was indeed the turn of a new century when I first gave Duncan a copy of the play. Some months later, in the wake of the shootings at Columbine, its subject felt all the more urgent; I approached (director) Michael Mayer about working on it with us.

These days, a short eight years later, in the shadow of the shootings at Virginia Tech, I am often asked why I ever thought *Spring Awakening* could work as a musical. And my only real answer is that I knew and loved the play, that I had long felt it was a sort of opera-in-waiting, and that somehow I could already "hear" Duncan's music in it.

Subtitled "A Children's Tragedy," Wedekind's play is full of the unheard, anguished cries of young people. It struck me that pop music—rock music—is the exact place that adolescents for the last few generations have found release from, and expression of, that same mute pain.

"The flesh has its own spirit," Wedekind once wrote. And surely his gorgeous threnody already has the soul of song within it. But I never dreamed that, by letting his characters actually sing, we would end up so profoundly transforming his work.

Then, perhaps there is something in the nature of song itself that opens the door to story—that admits us to the heart of the singer—as if every song tells of a sort of unacknowledged "I want." For, what we sing is what is unspoken, what is hidden. The "real story."

As we began work, I vowed to remain true to Wedekind's fierce original intent. But I soon found that once we had access, through song, to the inner workings of our characters' hearts and minds, we engaged with them differently—we embarked on journeys with them. Before long, we found ourselves altering the structure, even the substance, of our source material, to account for the places those songs had taken us.

From the start, my thought was that the songs in our show would function as interior monologues. Characters would not serenade one another in the middle of scenes. Rather, each student would give voice to his or her inner landscape.

Surely, the original play is full of exquisite monologues— a dramatic technique Wedekind inherited from his countrymen Goethe and Schiller. But our monologues were meant to be truly interior—a technique more familiar in twentieth-century fiction.

Instinctively, I felt I did not want to write lyrics which would forward the plot, and so chose not to follow that golden rule of musicals. I wanted a sharp and clear distinction between the world of the spoken and the world of the sung. And yet, I also wanted to create a seamless and ongoing musical counterpoint between the languages of those distinct worlds.

The infamous twentieth-century philosopher Ludwig Wittgenstein famously wrote: "What we cannot speak about, we must pass over in silence." And, yet, song seems to let us pause within that silence, to find ourselves articulate within it.

Within our show, the songs soon came to function as subtext. The boy and girl fumble to make polite conversation; but underneath, each of them already senses the enormous story about to unfold between them: "O, I'm gonna be wounded..."

We wrote songs as confession ("There is a part I can't tell, about the dark I know well"). Songs as denial ("Uh-huh, uh-huh, uh-huh... well, fine") or admission ("It's the bitch of living as someone you can't stand"). Songs as cri de coeur ("But there's nowhere to hide from the ghost in my mind..."). Somehow, I felt, we still remained true to that inchoate yearning of Wedekind's youths.

But of course we were also up to something else: in our show, the scenes set out the world of nineteenth-century repression, while the songs afford our young characters a momentary release into contemporary pop idiom. (Caught in the relentless dramas of our adolescent lives, we are all still rock stars in the privacy of our own bedrooms.) The time-jumping structure of our show is meant, thus, to underscore the sadly enduring relevance of our theme.

Some of my earliest efforts to transpose nineteenth-century yearnings into contemporary attitudes and idiom were fairly straightforward. A failure at school, a virtual pariah at home, stymied in his efforts to flee provincial Bavaria, Wedekind's Moritz wanders to the river at dusk and declares: "But then, it's better this way... I don't want to cry again— not today..." *Our* Moritz wanders into the same dusk, but soon ignites into neon—a post-punk kid at a mike who sings: "Awful sweet to be a little butterfly... 'Cause, you know, I don't do sadness..."

Certainly, my original vow was to remain true to Wedekind's text. Still, I have been alternately touched and bemused that so many critics have spoken so highly about how faithful we have been to the original, how admirably we have distilled it. *Maybe.* But, at the same time, we have fundamentally altered it. (I remember when Stephen Spinella, who joined our show just before our Broadway transfer, asked to see my uncut translation from Wedekind of several of his scenes. I had nothing to show him. He continued to press his suit: he really wanted to see Moritz's scene with his father in its longer form—a scene in which the man humiliates, strikes, and effectively renounces his son. Alas, I had to report that we never see Moritz with his father in the original play.)

Still, it has been more than merely adding new scenes, or thoroughly rewriting those already extant. We have created journeys for our three lead characters which do not exist in the original dark fractious fable.

As others have noted, the two biggest shifts we made to the tale occur at the ends of Act One and Act Two—in the hayloft and then in the graveyard. In Wedekind's script, Melchior "date-rapes" Wendla. We wanted to see him make love to her. More: we wanted to show how this young man (who jests at his friend's puberty wounds) first uncovers ineluctable sexual feelings; how he begins to own his sexual identity; how he helps Wendla awaken to hers. The truth is, we had already, irrevocably, set Melchior on this path when we gave him the song: "Touch Me." There, he articulates his sense of "the female" yearning for pleasure, singing as if in some hypothetical woman's voice: "Touch me, just like that. Now, there, *that's* it—God, that's heaven..." Sheltered in a hayloft in a rainstorm with an actual young woman— Wendla—and confronted with the possibility of *giving* her that pleasure, Melchior cannot restrain himself.

As for the graveyard... suffice it to say, after seven years' labor, we finally dispensed with the notorious Masked Man. This Symbolist figure appears—literally out of nowhere—in the last scene of Wedekind's text. He confronts the despairing Melchior and assures him that with a warm meal in his belly, he will no longer chafe to join his friend Moritz in the grave.

Without a doubt, this character is a sort of throwback, a deus ex machina, like those in Ancient Greek tragedies, who appear in the final scene to resolve the issues of the play. And yet, his appearance, along with the ghost of Moritz, who rises from his grave to tempt Melchior to suicide, effectively marks the birth of the Expressionist Theater (a world where iconic figures body forth the emotions of the central characters).

Since high school—when I first read the play—I have been haunted by the Masked Man. I struggled so long to incorporate him into our show, offering him up in one incarnation after another: as a sort of somber emcee, as an ever-present silent specter, as an actor who (living or dead) somehow survived the Allied bombing of a German theater. But we finally realized that within our piece the music already performs the role of the Masked Man, for it gives our adolescent characters a voice to celebrate, to decry, to embrace the darker longings within them *as part of them*, rather than as something to run from or repress.

As for Moritz arising from his grave to tell Melchior how good the dead have it, hovering high above joy and despair... it just seemed wrong to us—a cop-out, for dramaturgic effect, on a character we cared about and had worked so hard to illuminate. In our show, we witness Mortitz's struggles at school and home first-hand; his devotion to Melchior is his sole anchor. In song after song, he utters heartfelt, would-be defiant cries of anguish at the world grown dark around him. In the Expressionist original, the Moritz we meet in the graveyard is largely an aspect of Melchior's feeling—a projection. But for us, he was still our gangly Eraserhead. We didn't want to see him extend a rotting hand in an effort to betray his friend.

And yet, it felt appropriate to hear from him again, and also from Wendla. The question was: what did *we* want to say? If the answer wasn't a "warm meal" in a young Bavarian belly, then how was Melchior to find the strength to go on? Ultimately, the lyrics—the message—of Melchior's final song, "Those You've Known," came to me while writing it. I found the lyrics telling me: it was the love still felt for those we have known that enables us to continue in the face of losing them.

Now we had the end of our tale: a boy left thoroughly distraught, his rebellious spirit broken by The System, somehow finds sustenance at the source of his sufferings. He has learned to learn from his heart.

If the lesson to be learned was of the heart, then it made sense that we would introduce Melchior as a guy with a naive rebellious pride in the power of his own mind. And so (working backward from that lesson learned by show's end), we wrote his opening number, "All That's Known":

> *All they say*
> *Is "Trust in What Is Written."*
> *Wars are made,*
> *And somehow that is wisdom.*
>
> *Thought is suspect,*
> *And money is their idol,*
> *And nothing is okay unless it's scripted in their Bible.*
>
> *But I know*
> *There's so much more to find—*
> *Just in looking through myself, and not at them.*
>
> *Still, I know*
> *To trust my own true mind,*
> *And to say: "There's a way through this..."*

The realization of how our story should begin led us to construct an entirely new opening scene for our young rebel—the Latin Class—which does not exist in the original. This scene allowed us to see the boys in school. It allowed us to introduce a world of repression, where students are struck for giving the wrong answers. It let us see Moritz floundering. Most important, it showed us Melchior standing up for his friend and defending him.

In contrast, we were clear from the beginning about how to launch Wendla's story, and "Mama Who Bore Me" was one of the first songs Duncan and I wrote. I always felt our show should begin with this determined young woman asking her mother how babies are born, only to be rebuffed, coddled with bourgeois evasion.

In the original, this classic scene falls in Act Two. Wendla has already met Melchior, has indeed already been beaten by him. Moving the scene to the top of the show allowed us to make a political point right from the start: the seeds of the entire "children's tragedy" are sown by this one willful act of silence— a parent failing to talk honestly to her child about sex.

I saw Wendla as a girl with a mission—a nineteenth-century teen with a quest that could also feel contemporary. Thwarted by her mother, she keeps looking for answers: she wants to know the world of her strange new body. Disturbed but also darkly intrigued to learn Martha's father beats her, Wendla turns, searchingly, to Melchior. In the original script, when she asks him to beat her, he is dumbstruck; all she can offer is that she has never been beaten, her entire life. When our Wendla asks Melchior to beat her, he demands: "How can you even want such a thing?" And she responds: "I've never felt... *anything.*"

As Wedekind scripted it, the hayloft scene is brief— startlingly brief. With next to no acknowledgment of the horrific beating Melchior has inflicted on her, Wendla kneels beside him in the hay, and he begins kissing her. A moment later, he forces himself on her. We worked hard to flesh out a fuller scene between them, to let our would-be lovers struggle to make sense of what they have so brutally done—to offer one another forgiveness, before they fall into each other's arms.

From the top of Act Two, we wanted to see Wendla confusedly awakening to her own womanhood, owning her lovemaking, claiming her part of the pleasure. Where Wedekind gives her an Ophelia-like morning after, our young heroine celebrates in song the sweet unknown world she's just discovered. The final arc of her journey, however, came late in the process. Our producer Tom Hulce felt, and repeatedly warned, that we were letting our sometime-fearless young woman conclude her story as a "victim," lamenting the incomprehensible news that she was with child. The problem was, we all loved her sad song, "Whispering." One day, Michael proposed we try intercutting that song with the scene between Melchior's parents that follows it. As Wendla discovers the consequences of her night with Melchior, the more progressive Gabors, hearing the same news, give up on their son and send him to a reformatory.

It was an inspired idea. Somehow, in cutting those scenes together, it became plain that, over the course of her song, Wendla could undergo a transformation. Her song would then play in counterpoint with their scene: as Frau Gabor bows to her sense of duty and condemns Melchior, Wendla sets aside her grief and trusts what her heart found with him. And so I rewrote the words of "Whispering"—what had been, from near the beginning, my favorite lyric:

> *See the sweetheart on his knees,*
> *So faithful and adoring.*
> *Says he loves her,*
> *So she lets him have her—*
> *Another summer's story...*

As the story of the song changed, this chorus became:

> *Had a sweetheart on his knees,*
> *So faithful and adoring.*
> *And he touched me,*
> *And I let him love me.*
> *So, let that be my story...*

While Moritz finally succumbs to the humiliations of society (he can no longer face the prospect of a world that brooks no failure), our Wendla chooses to remember the love she has felt, to ignore the ghostly whispers of society, and embrace the new life already whispering within her.

And with that move, our play made its pro-choice stance explicit. Wendla's abortion was, in a sense, transported into our own century: a century in which a "bourgeois idea" such as abstinence is still widely preached as the only form of safe sex; where the widespread dissemination of contraceptive devices is described by some within our Department of Health and Human Services as demeaning to women. One can only hope that a century from now the world will finally hear, and honestly answer, the cries of its Wendlas.

And so I am left pondering how and why all this ever came to be. I remember the first time I walked by our marquee, feeling almost baffled: "*Spring Awakening—A Musical*? Wait, no, isn't that just the name of a book in my room?"

I can honestly say that my earliest sense of why this "kindertragodie" could work as a piece of musical theater was instinctual. Even so, the entire eight-year siege of developing it entailed nothing harder than learning to trust our instincts. As Michael has recently said, we didn't set out to "revolutionize the musical theater," nor with the express intention of doing something different. Rather, we had a story we wanted to tell, and a way we all felt we wanted to tell it.

Through all those years, through the darkest hours when our project fell off almost everyone's radar, Michael never lost heart, never lost faith in our ability to pull the thing together. For all the endless nights he spent going through line after line, every syllable of this text with me... well, this text—the show itself—are all I have to repay that.

As for the debt to Duncan... who can explain the mystic thing that happens when I hand him a lyric and he somehow hears a song in it. When (in a moment indelibly etched in my memory) he first looks through those words, picks up his guitar and strums: "There's a moment you know..." And then he pauses, looks up with a grin, and sings: "you're fucked."

S.S.
New York
May 2007

SPRING AWAKENING
A MUSICAL

Over the years of its development, *Spring Awakening* profited from a number of workshops, each one directed by Michael Mayer. The first was in September 1999: a four-day rehearsed reading at La Jolla Playhouse, at Annie Hamburger's invitation. A three-week workshop at the Sundance Theatre Lab followed, in the summer of 2000. In December 2000, the piece had a two-week workshop, culminating in an unstaged reading, at the Roundabout Theatre Company (the then fourteen-year-old Lea Michele joined the company as Wendla). In June 2001, the show enjoyed a second workshop at the Roundabout. Sadly, scheduled productions at both the Roundabout and the Long Wharf Theatre (for the 2001–2002 and 2002–2003 seasons) fell apart. It was not until February 2005 that, with the help of producer Tom Hulce, the show was workshopped again: a concert reading in the Allen Room for Lincoln Center's "American Songbook" series (John Gallagher, Jr., and Skylar Astin were featured, along with Lea). In March 2006, *Spring Awakening* received its sixth, and final, workshop at Baruch College, under the auspices of the Atlantic Theater Company.

The world premiere production of *Spring Awakening* was produced in New York City at the Atlantic Theater Company (Neil Pepe, Artistic Director; Andrew D. Hamingson, Managing Director), in association with Tom Hulce and Ira Pittelman, on June 15, 2006. It was directed by Michael Mayer; choreography was by Bill T. Jones, scenic design was by Christine Jones, lighting design was by Kevin Adams, costume design was by Susan Hilferty, sound design was by Brian Ronan, the string arrangements were by Simon Hale, the vocal arrangements were by AnnMarie Milazzo; the musical director was Kimberly Grigsby and the production stage manager was Allison Sommers. The band included: Thad DeBrock, guitar; George Farmer, bass; Trey Files, percussion and Benjamin Kalb, cello. The cast was as follows:

The Girls

WENDLA	Lea Michele
MARTHA	Lilli Cooper
THEA	Remy Zaken
ANNA	Phoebe Strole
ILSE	Lauren Pritchard

The Boys

MELCHIOR	Jonathan Groff
MORITZ	John Gallagher, Jr.
HANSCHEN / RUPERT	Jonathan B. Wright
ERNST / REINHOLD	Gideon Glick
GEORG / DIETER	Skylar Astin
OTTO / ULBRECHT	Brian Charles Johnson

The Adult Women   Mary McCann

FRAU BERGMAN, Wendla's mother
FRAU GABOR, Melchior's mother
FRAU BESSELL, Martha's mother
FRAULEIN KNUPPELDICK
FRAULEIN GROSSEBUSTENHALTER

The Adult Men   Frank Wood

HERR GABOR, Melchior's father
HERR STIEFEL, Moritz's father
HERR RILOW, Hanschen's father
HERR NEUMANN, Ilse's father
HERR SONNENSTICH

HEADMASTER KNOCHENBRUCH
FATHER KAULBACH
DOCTOR VON BRAUSEPULVER
SCHMIDT

Spring Awakening moved to Broadway at the Eugene O'Neill Theatre (A Jujamcyn Theatre: Rocco Landesman, President; Paul Libin, Producing Director; Jack Viertel, Creative Director), opening on December 10, 2006. It was produced by the Atlantic Theater Company, Tom Hulce, Ira Pittelman, Jeffrey Richards, Jerry Frankel, Jeffrey Sine, Freddy DeMann, Max Cooper, Mort Swinsky, Cindy and Jay Gutterman, Joe McGinnis, Judith Ann Abrams, ZenDog Productions, CarJac Productions, Aron Bergson Productions, Jennifer Manocherian, Ted Snowdon, Harold Thau, Terry Schnuck, Cold Spring Productions, Amanda Dubois, Elizabeth Eynon Wetherell, Jennifer Maloney, Tamara Tunie, Joe Cilibrasi and StyleFour Productions. It was directed by Michael Mayer; choreography was by Bill T. Jones, scenic design was by Christine Jones, lighting design was by Kevin Adams, costume design was by Susan Hilferty, sound design was by Brian Ronan, the orchestrations were by Duncan Sheik, the string arrangements were by Simon Hale, the vocal arrangements were by AnnMarie Milazzo; the musical director was Kimberly Grigsby, the production stage manager was Heather Cousens and the stage manager was Rick Steiger. The band included: Kimberly Grigsby, conductor/keyboards; Thad DeBrock, guitar; George Farmer, bass; Trey Files, associate conductor/percussion; Benjamin Kalb, cello; Olivier Manchon, violin/guitar and Hiroko Taguchi, viola. The cast was as follows:

The Girls

WENDLA	Lea Michele
MARTHA	Lilli Cooper
THEA	Remy Zaken
ANNA	Phoebe Strole
ILSE	Lauren Pritchard

The Boys

MELCHIOR
MORITZ
HANSCHEN / RUPERT
ERNST / REINHOLD
GEORG / DIETER
OTTO / ULBRECHT

Jonathan Groff
John Gallagher, Jr.
Jonathan B. Wright
Gideon Glick
Skylar Astin
Brian Charles Johnson

The Adult Women

Christine Estabrook

FRAU BERGMAN, Wendla's mother
FRAU GABOR, Melchior's mother
FRAU BESSELL, Martha's mother
FRAULEIN KNUPPELDICK
FRAULEIN GROSSEBUSTENHALTER

The Adult Men

Stephen Spinella

HERR GABOR, Melchior's father
HERR STIEFEL, Moritz's father
HERR RILOW, Hanschen's father
HERR NEUMANN, Ilse's father
HERR SONNENSTICH
HEADMASTER KNOCHENBRUCH
FATHER KAULBACH
DOCTOR VON BRAUSEPULVER
SCHMIDT

Ensemble

Gerard Canonico
Jennifer Damiano
Robert Hager
Krysta Rodriguez

Spring Awakening received its British premiere at the Lyric Hammersmith, London, on January 23, 2009, before transferring to the Novello Theatre in the West End on March 21, 2009. It was directed by Michael Mayer, choreography was by Bill T. Jones, scenic design was by Christine Jones, lighting design was by Kevin Adams, costume design was by Susan Hilferty, sound design was by Brian Ronan, casting was by Pippa Ailion CDG, the orchestrations were by Duncan Sheik and Simon Hale, the vocal arrangements were by AnnMarie Milazzo, the musical supervisor was Kimberly Grigsby, and the musical director was Nigel Lilley. The cast was as follows:

The Girls

WENDLA	Charlotte Wakefield
MARTHA	Hayley Gallivan
THEA	Evelyn Hoskins
ANNA	Natasha Barnes
ILSE	Lucy May Barker

The Boys

MELCHIOR	Aneurin Barnard
MORITZ	Iwan Rheon
HANSCHEN / RUPERT	Jamie Blackley
ERNST / REINHOLD	Harry McEntire
GEORG / DIETER	Jos Slovick
OTTO / ULBRECHT	Edd Judge

The Adult Women   Sian Thomas

The Adult Men   Richard Cordery

Ensemble   Chris Barton
Natalie Garner
Mona Goodwin
Jamie Muscato
Gemma O'Duffy
Richard Southgate

Spring Awakening was revived at the Almeida Theatre, London, on December 7, 2021. It was directed by Rupert Goold, choreography was by Lynne Page, set design was by Miriam Buether, costume design was by Nicky Gillibrand, lighting design was by Jack Knowles, sound design was by Tony Gayle, video design was by Finn Ross, the orchestrations were by Duncan Sheik and Simon Hale, the musical director was Jo Cichonska, orchestral management was by David Gallagher and Justin Pearson, the intimacy director was Ita O'Brien, the casting directors were Pippa Ailion CDG and Natalie Gallacher CDG, and the fight director was Bret Yount. The cast was as follows:

The Girls

WENDLA	Amara Okereke
MARTHA	Bella Maclean
THEA	Asha Banks
ANNA	Maia Tamrakar
ILSE	Carly-Sophia Davies
CLARA	Emily Ooi

The Boys

MELCHIOR	Laurie Kynaston
MORITZ	Stuart Thompson
HANSCHEN / RUPERT	Nathan Armarkwei-Laryea
ERNST / REINHOLD	Zheng Xi Yong
GEORG / DIETER	Joe Pitts
OTTO / ULBRECHT	Kit Esuruoso
FRANK / KARL	Taylor Bradshaw

The Adult Women	Catherine Cusack
The Adult Men	Mark Lockyer
Swings	Tom Grant
	Mali O'Donnell

PAGE ONE

Lea Michele (Wendla) and Jonathan Groff (Melchior) in the original Broadway production at the Eugene O'Neill Theatre, New York City, December 2006.
(Photo: Joan Marcus/ArenaPAL)

PAGE TWO

Aneurin Barnard (Melchior) and Charlotte Wakefield (Wendla) in the original London production at the Lyric Hammersmith, January 2009.
(Photo: Nigel Norrington/ArenaPAL)

PAGE THREE

Left to right: Edd Judge (Otto), Jamie Blackley (Hanschen), Jos Slovick (Georg) and Aneurin Barnard (Melchior) in the original London production at the Lyric Hammersmith, January 2009.
(Photo: Geraint Lewis/ArenaPAL)

PAGE FOUR

Centre: Austin P. McKenzie (Melchior) and the cast in Deaf West Theatre's Broadway revival at the Brooks Atkinson Theatre, New York City, September 2015.
(Photo: Joan Marcus/ArenaPAL)

The Girls

WENDLA
MARTHA
THEA
ANNA
ILSE

The Boys

MELCHIOR
MORITZ
HANSCHEN / RUPERT
ERNST / REINHOLD
GEORG / DIETER
OTTO / ULBRECHT

The Adult Women (played by one woman)

FRAU BERGMAN, Wendla's mother
FRAU GABOR, Melchior's mother
FRAU BESSELL, Martha's mother
FRAULEIN KNUPPELDICK
FRAULEIN GROSSEBUSTENHALTER

The Adult Men (played by one man)

HERR GABOR, Melchior's father
HERR STIEFEL, Moritz's father
HERR RILOW, Hanschen's father

HERR NEUMANN, Ilse's father
HERR SONNENSTICH
HEADMASTER KNOCHENBRUCH
FATHER KAULBACH
DOCTOR VON BRAUSEPULVER
SCHMIDT

The action of the play is set in a provincial German town in the late nineteenth century. When singing, however, the Boys and Girls assume the manner of contemporary teens. The lights shift with the songs, and we enter the private and timeless world of the character who is singing. That character may be joined in his or her solitary song by other voices that fill out the chorus of longing.

From the inception of this project, Duncan, Michael and I imagined that when the characters broke out of their nineteenth-century confines, they would pull hand mikes from their pockets and rock out. And indeed, that is just what they've done, to great effect, in both our New York productions.

Seeing "the kids" step into a spotlight in period costume and sing mike in hand, or from behind a mike stand, has been dynamic. It has given us a visual embodiment, a clear signal, of the break between our bourgeois German province and our alt-rock concert.

Though this script is divided into many scenes, I always imagined that the play would unfold with great fluidity: a minimal amount of transition, as one moment morphs into the next. Given that the show also shifts continually between scene and song worlds, it made real sense to play on a near-empty stage, with a nonrepresentational set. Lighting, then, became the thing.

On that front, too, we had a strong idea: our young characters live in the shadow of social convention, but their inner worlds are utterly electric. And, the effect of a sudden break from a world lit by lanterns to one ignited by neon has been pretty spectacular.

Finally, in our staging, all of the characters have remained present and visible throughout the show. This has greatly facilitated the entrances and exits of the chorus of Boys and Girls into and out of the songs.

But I offer these thoughts only as notes from our journal. I am genuinely excited to see how others choose to address the potentially tricky staging issues raised by this most-particular, and long-begotten, text.

*Costume
sketches by
Susan Hilferty:
Melchior and
Wendla (top),
Moritz
(bottom).*

Ilse, Martha, Thea and Anna (clockwise, from top left).

Hanschen, Ernst, Otto and Georg (clockwise, from top left).

ACT ONE

SCENE 1

Wendla is revealed in song light, as if at a mirror. She gently explores her newly maturing body, pulls on a near-transparent schoolgirl dress.

WENDLA:
> *Mama who bore me.*
> *Mama who gave me*
> *No way to handle things. Who made me so sad.*
>
> *Mama, the weeping.*
> *Mama, the angels.*
> *No sleep in Heaven, or Bethlehem.*
>
> *Some pray that, one day, Christ will come a-callin'.*
> *They light a candle, and hope that it glows.*
> *And some just lie there, crying for him to come and find them.*
> *But when he comes, they don't know how to go...*
>
> *Mama who bore me.*
> *Mama who gave me*
> *No way to handle things. Who made me so bad.*

Mama, the weeping.
Mama, the angels.
No sleep in Heaven, or Bethlehem.

(The lights shift to the world of 1891: a provincial German living room. Frau Bergman suddenly enters, beaming.)

FRAU BERGMAN: Wendla!

WENDLA: Mama?

FRAU BERGMAN: Goodness, look at you—in that... that kindergarten dress! Wendla, grown-up girls cannot be seen strutting about in such—

WENDLA: Let me wear this one, Mama! I love this one. It makes me feel like a little... faerie-queen.

FRAU BERGMAN: But you're already... in bloom.

(Off her look) Now, sssh. You made me forget all our good news.

Just imagine, Wendla, last night the stork finally visited your sister. Brought her another little baby girl.

WENDLA: I can't wait to see her, Mama.

FRAU BERGMAN: Well, put on a proper dress, and take a hat.

(Wendla starts out, hesitates.)

WENDLA: Mama, don't be cross—don't be. But I'm an aunt for the second time now, and I still have no idea how it happens.

(Frau Bergman looks stricken.)

Mama, please. I'm ashamed to even ask. But then, who can I ask but you?

FRAU BERGMAN: Wendla, child, you cannot imagine that I could—

WENDLA: But you cannot imagine I still believe in the stork.

FRAU BERGMAN: I honestly don't know what I've done to deserve this kind of talk. And on a day like today!

Go, child, put your clothes on.

WENDLA: And if I run out, now, and ask Gregor? Our chimney sweep...?

(A beat.)

FRAU BERGMAN: Very well, I'll tell you everything.
    But not today. Tomorrow. Or the day after.
WENDLA: Today, Mama.
FRAU BERGMAN: Wendla Bergman, I simply cannot...
WENDLA: Mama!
FRAU BERGMAN: You will drive me mad.
WENDLA: Why? I'll kneel at your feet, lay my head in your lap... You can talk as if I weren't even here.

(No response.)

Please.
FRAU BERGMAN: Very well, I'll tell you.

(Wendla kneels. Flustered, Frau Bergman buries the girl's head in her apron.)

WENDLA *(Waits)*: Yes?...
FRAU BERGMAN: Child, I...
WENDLA: Mama.
FRAU BERGMAN: All right, then. In order for a woman to conceive a child...
    You follow me?
WENDLA: Yes, Mama.
FRAU BERGMAN: For a woman to bear a child, she must... in her own personal way, she must... love her husband. Love him, as she can love only him. *Only* him... she must love— with her whole... heart.
    There. Now, you know everything.
WENDLA: Everything?...
FRAU BERGMAN *("Yes")*: Everything. So help me.
WENDLA *(Not budging)*: Mama!

(The lights shift—we are back in the song world. Contemporary music sounds. The Girls appear. Wendla rises and joins them. Shedding her nineteenth-century formality, she sings, as do all the Girls, in the manner of a contemporary young woman.)

WENDLA AND GIRLS:
>*Mama who bore me.*
>*Mama who gave me*
>*No way to handle things. Who made me so sad.*
>
>*Mama, the weeping.*
>*Mama, the angels.*
>*No sleep in Heaven, or Bethlehem.*
>
>*Some pray that, one day, Christ will come a-callin'.*
>*They light a candle, and hope that it glows.*
>*And some just lie there, crying for him to come and find*
>   *them.*
>*But when he comes, they don't know how to go...*
>
>*Mama who bore me.*
>*Mama who gave me*
>*No way to handle things. Who made me so bad.*
>
>*Mama, the weeping.*
>*Mama, the angels.*
>*No sleep in Heaven, or Bethlehem.*

SCENE 2

School. The Boys sit upright at their desks, reciting from Virgil's
Aeneid. They stand, one after the other, for their recitation. Herr
Sonnenstich walks the aisles beside them, listening.

HERR SONNENSTICH: Again.

OTTO *(Mid-recitation)*:
>...vi superum saevae memorem Iunonis ob iram...

HERR SONNENSTICH *("Well done")*: Better, Herr
Lammermeier. Continue, Herr Zirschnitz.

GEORG:
>...multa quoque et bello passus, dum conderet urbem.

HERR SONNENSTICH: Herr Rilow. From the beginning.

HANSCHEN:
>Arma virumque cano, Troiae qui primus ab oris—

HERR SONNENSTICH: Herr Robel. And...

ERNST:
>...Italiam, fato profugus, Laviniaque venit
>litora—

HERR SONNENSTICH: Herr Stiefel.

(But, alas, Moritz is asleep.)

Herr Stiefel.
MORITZ *(Waking)*: Sir?...
HERR SONNENSTICH: Continue. Please. *(Moritz hesitates)*
Herr Stiefel...

MORITZ *(Haltingly)*:
>...Laviniaque venit...

HERR SONNENSTICH: Yes...?

MORITZ:
>...litora... multum enim—

HERR SONNENSTICH: "Multum *enim*"?

MORITZ *(Taking another stab at it)*:
>...multum *olim*—

HERR SONNENSTICH *(Losing patience)*: *"Olim"?!* "Multum *olim*"...?! So then, somehow the Pious Aeneas has *"already"* suffered much "in the days still to come"...?

(No response.)

Herr Stiefel?

(No response.)

Do you have any idea what you're saying, Herr Stiefel?

(Moritz is too mortified to respond. Melchior rises.)

MELCHIOR: If you please!

HERR SONNENSTICH: Pardon me?

MELCHIOR *(Covering gracefully)*: If you please, Herr Sonnenstich... can't we at least consider "multum olim" as a plausible conjecture for how the text might read?

HERR SONNENSTICH: Herr Gabor. We are hardly here today to conjecture about textual conjectures. The boy has made an error.

MELCHIOR: Yes. But an understandable error, sir. Indeed, if we could only entertain the fitness of the conjecture—

HERR SONNENSTICH: "Multum *olim*"?!

MELCHIOR: Look to the fresh rhetorical balance—"*multum olim*" introducing "*multa* quoque"—a parallel, sir, between what Aeneas has already suffered in war and those sufferings on land and sea just ahead.

HERR SONNENSTICH: Herr Gabor, since the days of Servius, Aulus Gellius, and Claudius Donatus—nay, since the moment of Virgil's death—our world has been littered with more than sufficient critical commentary on textual conjecture.

MELCHIOR: With all respect, sir, are you then suggesting there is no further room for critical thought or interpretation? Why indeed, then, do we even—

HERR SONNENSTICH *(Striking Melchior with his teacher's cane)*: I am suggesting no such thing. I am confirming that Herr Stiefel has made an error. And I am asking—nay, demanding—that you emend his faulty text and proceed from there. Do I make myself clear?

(Melchior's jaw locks.)

Herr Gabor?

(No response. He strikes Melchior more forcefully.)

Herr Gabor, do I make myself clear?

MELCHIOR: Yes, Herr Sonnenstich: "litora multum ille."

HERR SONNENSTICH: All of you—together with Melchior Gabor:

"Laviniaque venit..."

BOYS:

...litora, multum ille et terris iactatus et alto
vi superum saevae memorem Iunonis ob...

(The Boys' recitation grows louder, more insistent, more numbing—as if somehow we were entering into Melchior's psychic experience of it. A bit of contemporary, electronic music drifts through. Shimmering song light finds Melchior. He turns out and sings—like a rocker in concert:)

MELCHIOR:

All that's known
In History, in Science,
Overthrown
At school, at home,
    by blind men.

You doubt them,
And soon they bark
    and hound you—
Till everything you say
    is just another bad
    about you.

All they say
Is, "Trust in What Is
    Written."
Wars are made,
And somehow that is
    wisdom.

Thought is suspect,
And money is their idol,
And nothing is okay unless it's scripted in their Bible.

BOYS:

...iram;
multa quoque et bello
    passus, dum conderet
    urbem...

Arma virumque cano, Troiae
    qui primus ab oris
Italiam, fato profugus,
    Laviniaque venit
litora, multum ille et terris
    iactatus et alto
vi superum saevae memorem

Iunonis ob iram;
multa quoque et bello
    passus, dum conderet
    urbem...

But I know
There's so much more to find—
Just in looking through myself, and not at them.

Still, I know
To trust my own true mind,
And to say: "There's a way through this..."

On I go,
To wonder and to learning—
Name the stars and know their dark returning.

I'm calling,
To know the world's true yearning—
The hunger that a child feels for everything they're shown.

You watch me—
Just watch me—
I'm calling,
And one day all will know...

You watch me—
Just watch me—
I'm calling,
I'm calling,
And one day all will know...

(Melchior's song concludes. As he rejoins the Boys in their recitation, the lights shift back to the classroom.)

BOYS AND MELCHIOR:
  ...multa quoque et bello passus, dum conderet urbem...

HERR SONNENSTICH *(On to fresh matters)*: Thank you, gentlemen. Now, if you please: "inferretque deos Latio..." The *following* seven lines of Pious Aeneas' journey. From memory.

(The Boys begin scribbling. Herr Sonnenstich steps away. Moritz taps Melchior's shoulder.)

MORITZ *(Sotto voce)*: Melchi, thank you.

MELCHIOR: It's nothing.

MORITZ: Still, I'm sorry. You didn't need to—

MELCHIOR *("Not to worry"; ironic)*: Think what Aeneas suffered.

MORITZ: But I should have known it. "Multum ille." It's just...
I didn't sleep all night. In fact, I, uh, suffered a visit from
the most horrific, dark phantasm...

MELCHIOR: You mean, a dream?...

MORITZ: A nightmare, really. Legs in sky blue stockings,
climbing over the lecture podium.

MELCHIOR: Oh. *That* kind of dream.

MORITZ *("Indeed")*: Have you ever suffered such... mortifying
visions?

MELCHIOR: Moritz, of course. We all have. Otto
Lammermeier dreamt about his mother.

MORITZ: Really?!!

MELCHIOR: Georg Zirschnitz? Dreamt he was seduced by his
piano teacher.

MORITZ: Fraulein Grossebustenhalter?!

HERR SONNENSTICH *(Suddenly, grabbing Moritz by the ear)*:
Moritz Stiefel. I need hardly remind you that, of all our
pupils, *you* are in no position to be taking liberties. I will
not warn you again.

*(Moritz nods—absolutely petrified. An intense alt-rock guitar
riff. Herr Sonnenstich freezes. The world around Moritz comes
to a halt as concert-like light finds him. He turns out in song:)*

MORITZ:

> *God, I dreamed there was an angel, who could hear me
>   through the wall,*
> *As I cried out—like, in Latin: "This is so not life at all.*
> *Help me out—out—of this nightmare." Then I heard her
>   silver call—*
> *She said: "Just give it time, kid. I come to one and all."*
>
> *She said: "Give me that hand, please, and the itch you
>   can't control,*
> *Let me teach you how to handle all the sadness in your soul.*

Oh, we'll work that silver magic, then we'll aim it at the
 wall."
She said: "Love may make you blind, kid—but I wouldn't
 mind at all."

*(All the Boys except Melchior begin to move, joining Moritz
one by one, their energy building into a dance.)*

MORITZ AND BOYS:
 It's the bitch of living
 With nothing but your hand.
 Just the bitch of living
 As someone you can't stand...

GEORG:
 See, each night, it's, like, fantastic—tossing, turning,
 without rest,
 'Cause my day's at the piano—with my teacher and her
 breasts;
 And the music's, like, the one thing I can even get at all,
 And those breasts! I mean, God, please, just let those
 apples fall...

BOYS:
 It's the bitch of living
 With nothing going on.
 Just the bitch of living,
 Asking: "What went wrong?"

 Do they think we want this?
 Oh—who knows?

ERNST:
 See, there's showering in gym class...

HANSCHEN:
 Bobby Maler, he's the best—
 Looks so nasty in those khakis...

ERNST:
>   *God, my whole life's, like, some test.*

OTTO:
>   *Then there's Marianna Wheelan—as if she'd return my call.*

HANSCHEN:
>   *It's like, just kiss some ass, man—then you can screw
>   'em all.*

(Melchior joins the song.)

MELCHIOR:
>   *It's the bitch of living—*
>   *And living in your head.*
>   *It's the bitch of living,*
>   *And sensing God is dead.*

MORITZ AND BOYS:
>   *It's the bitch of living*
>   *And trying to get ahead.*
>   *It's the bitch of living—*

MELCHIOR:
>   *You watch me—*
>   *Just watch me—*
>   *I'm calling,*
>   *And one day all will*
>   *know...*

MORITZ:
>   *Just getting out of bed.*

MORITZ AND BOYS:
>   *It's the bitch of living—*
>   *And getting what you get.*
>   *Just the bitch of living—*

MELCHIOR:
>   *And knowing this is it.*

MELCHIOR, MORITZ AND BOYS:
>   *God, is this it?*
>   *This can't be it.*
>   *Oh God, what a bitch!*

(The song ends. The lights shift back. The school day resumes.)

HERR SONNENSTICH: Gentlemen, turn in your verses, and clear away your personal effects. I will see you tomorrow, seven a.m.

(Herr Sonnenstich goes out. The Boys gather their books.)

OTTO *(Heading out)*: Well, I'm off.

ERNST: Me, too.

HANSCHEN: I'll walk with you, Ernst.

ERNST *(Pauses, turns back)*: You will?

HANSCHEN *("Yes"; suggestively)*: We'll huddle over the Homer. Maybe do a little Achilles and Patroclus...

(Hanschen leads Ernst off.)

GEORG *("Good night")*: Melchior, Moritz.

MELCHIOR *(Archly)*: Home to Bach?...

GEORG: Fraulein Grossebustenhalter will not be kept waiting.

(Georg shivers involuntarily, and goes. Melchior turns to Moritz with a wink, but Moritz waves it away.)

MORITZ: Ach, Melchi! Sixty lines of Homer, all those quadratic equations... I'll be up all night again, haunted by another of those... dreams. And still I won't get through it.

MELCHIOR: Oh, yes. Your dream.

MORITZ *("The horror!")*: Melchi, why—why—am I haunted by the legs of a woman? By the deepening conviction: some dark part of my destiny may lie there between them?...

MELCHIOR: All right then. I'll tell you. I got it out of books. But prepare yourself: it made an atheist out of me.

(A beat.)

So—

MORITZ: No no—not here! I can't talk it! No—do me a favor: write it down. *All* of it. Conceal it in my satchel—after Gymnastics—tomorrow.

(A beat.)

If you like, you could add some illustrations in the margins.

(A beat.)

MELCHIOR: Top to bottom?
MORITZ: *Everything.*

(Headmaster Knochenbruch and his associate, Fraulein Knuppeldick, stroll past and pause.)

HERR KNOCHENBRUCH: Unfathomable. Fraulein Knuppeldick.
FRAULEIN KNUPPELDICK: Herr Knochenbruch...?
HERR KNOCHENBRUCH: Look at that. Melchior Gabor, a young man of distinct intellectual capability—
FRAULEIN KNUPPELDICK: Thoroughly distinct.
HERR KNOCHENBRUCH: A young man who could be our finest pupil—
FRAULEIN KNUPPELDICK: Our finest, Herr Knochenbruch.
HERR KNOCHENBRUCH: But there he is, polluting himself, cavorting about with that, that...
FRAULEIN KNUPPELDICK: Neurasthenic imbecile, Moritz Stiefel?
HERR KNOCHENBRUCH: Thank Heaven the upper grade only holds sixty.

(Herr Knochenbruch and Fraulein Knuppeldick go off.)

SCENE 3

Late afternoon. A bridge in the countryside. Wendla, Martha, Thea and Anna walk home, talking excitedly.

THEA *(Mid-conversation):*... And the bodice in lace, with a satin bow in back...
ANNA: *Ooh!* And Wendla—what will you wear to Greta Brandenburg's wedding?
WENDLA: Mama said we cannot go.

THEA: To Greta's wedding?!

MARTHA: Because she's marrying that forest inspector?

WENDLA: Mama felt it was a little improper.

ANNA: But, they're decking the entire sanctuary in orchids and chrysanthemums!...

WENDLA: Mama said no.

(Anna and Thea exchange a look.)

ANNA: I certainly hope your mama approves the man I marry.

THEA: And the man *I* marry!

WENDLA *(Teasing)*: Well, we all know who Thea longs to marry!

MARTHA: Melchior Gabor!

THEA *("Gimme a break")*: And who doesn't?

ANNA *(Still playful)*: He is rather handsome...

WENDLA: So wonderful.

MARTHA *(Her secret crush)*: But not *so* wonderful as that sad soulful sleepyhead, Moritz Stiefel...

ANNA AND THEA: Moritz Stiefel!?

THEA: How can you even compare them? Melchi Gabor, he's such a radical. You know what the whisper is?

(All the Girls lean in, eager to hear.)

He doesn't believe in anything. Not in God.

(The Girls gasp in wonder.)

Not in Heaven.

(Another gasp.)

Not in a single thing in this world.

(The Girls utter a final, collective sigh.)

ANNA: They say he's the best, in everything. Latin, Greek, Trigonometry...

THEA: The best part is: he doesn't care a whit about any of it...

(*Music begins—an innocent uptempo feel. The Girls turn out—glistening in girl-group light:*)

WENDLA:
> *In the midst of this nothing, this miss of a life,*
> *Still, there's this one thing—just to see you go by.*

MARTHA:
> *It's almost like lovin'—sad as that is.*

THEA:
> *May not be cool, but it's so where I live.*

ANNA:
> *It's like I'm your lover—or, more like your ghost—*
> *I spend the day wonderin' what you do, where you go...*

THEA:
> *I try and just kick it, but then, what can I do?*
> *We've all got our junk, and my junk is you.*

GIRLS:
> *See us winter walkin'—after a storm.*
> *It's chill in the wind—but it's warm in your arms.*
> *We stop, all snow blind—may not be true.*
> *But we've all got our junk, and my junk is you.*

(*The lights shift, revealing Georg at his piano. Fraulein Grossebustenhalter hovers.*)

FRAULEIN GROSSEBUSTENHALTER: Well done, Georg. And now, the Prelude in C Minor...

(*Georg begins playing Bach's Prelude. As he does, Fraulein Grossebustenhalter touches his hand. He lets out an illicit sigh—a moment of private bliss. The lights shift, revealing Hanschen seated in his bathroom, wearing his nightshirt. He pulls a reproduction of Correggio's Io from his pocket. His free hand sneaks under his nightshirt.*)

HANSCHEN *(To Io/Desdemona)*: Have you prayed tonight, Desdemona? You don't look like you're praying, darling—lying there, contemplating the coming bliss...

(A knocking on the door. Hanschen freezes.)

HERR RILOW: Hanschen, you all right?
HANSCHEN: My stomach again, Father. But I'll be fine.
HERR RILOW: Yes?
HANSCHEN: Fine.
HERR RILOW: Well, then.

(Herr Rilow goes. Slowly and steadily, Hanschen begins to masturbate—building steam as the scene continues.)

HANSCHEN *(To Io/Desdemona)*: Darling, don't think I take your murder lightly. The truth is, I can hardly bear to think of the long nights ahead... But it's sucking the marrow from my bones, seeing you lie there. Motionless. Staring at me, so innocently. One of us must go—it's you or me.

(The lights shift... Fraulein Grossebustenhalter sternly interrupts Georg's playing.)

FRAULEIN GROSSEBUSTENHALTER: No, no! Georg, please. Again. And this time, bring out the left hand.

(Fraulein Grossebustenhalter touches his hand again—double the bliss.
Hanschen dutifully switches hands—to the left.)

HANSCHEN: Darling, why—why—do you press your knees together? Even now, on the brink of eternity? Don't you see it's your terrible chastity that's driving me to...

(A knocking at the bathroom door. Hanschen freezes.)

HERR RILOW: Hanschen, that's enough in there.
HANSCHEN: Yes, sir.

HERR RILOW: Back to bed.

(Hanschen does not move.)

Son?
HANSCHEN: One minute.

(Hanschen waits, listening. Herr Rilow goes. Hanschen redoubles his exertions.)

One last kiss. Those soft, white thighs... those girlish breasts... O, those cruel cruel knees...

(Fraulein Grossebustenhalter claps, interrupting Georg's playing.)

FRAULEIN GROSSEBUSTENHALTER: Répétez, s'il vous plaît.

(Georg turns out and sings. We enter the world of his fantasy.)

GEORG:
>*Well, you'll have to excuse me, I know it's so off,*
>*I love when you do stuff that's rude and so wrong.*

(Fraulein Grossebustenhalter rips open her bodice, exposing her bustier. Georg beckons her onto his lap and fondles her. As he does, Hanschen turns out, in a world of his own:)

HANSCHEN:
>*I go up to my room, turn the stereo on,*
>*Shoot up some you in the "you" of some song.*

(The Girls surround Hanschen, dancing. Oblivious to their charms, he only has eyes—and thumbs—for his Io. The Boys join in, as a vocal chorus:)

GIRLS, MORITZ, GEORG AND OTTO:
>*I lie back, just driftin', and play out these scenes.*
>*I ride on the rush—all the hopes, all the dreams...*

ANNA:

> *I may be neglectin' the things I should do.*
> *We've all got our junk, and my junk is you.*

BOYS AND GIRLS:

> *See, we still keep talkin'—after you're gone.*
> *You're still with me then—feels so good in my arms.*
> *They say you go blind—maybe it's true.*
> *But we've all got our junk, and my junk is you...*

> *(As the song reaches a climax, so does Hanschen.)*

> *It's like, we stop time. What can I do—*
> *We've all got our junk, and my junk is you.*

> *And my junk is you—*
> *You—you—you.*

SCENE 4

Evening. Melchior's study. A lamp burning on the table. Melchior sits alone, writing in his journal.

MELCHIOR *(Reading aloud as he writes)*: 16 October. The question is: Shame. What is its origin? And why are we hounded by its miserable shadow?

Does the mare feel Shame as she couples with a stallion? Are they deaf to everything their loins are telling them, until we grant them a marriage certificate? I think not.

To my mind, Shame is nothing but a product of Education. Meanwhile, old Father Kaulbach still blindly insists, in every single sermon, that it's deeply rooted in our sinful Human Nature. Which is why I now refuse to go to Church—

FRAU GABOR *(From off)*: Melchior?

MELCHIOR: Yes, Mama?

FRAU GABOR *(From off)*: Moritz Stiefel to see you.

(Melchior sits up. Moritz enters, looking pale and agitated.)

MELCHIOR: Moritz?...

MORITZ: Sorry I'm so late. I yanked on a jacket, ran a brush through my hair, and dashed like some phantom to get here.

MELCHIOR: You slept through the day?...

MORITZ *("Yes")*: I'm exhausted, Melchi. I was up till three in the morning—reading that essay you gave me, till I couldn't see straight.

MELCHIOR: Sit. Let me roll you a smoke.

(Melchior rolls Moritz a cigarette.)

MORITZ: Look at me—I'm trembling. Last night I prayed like Christ in Gethsemane: "Please, God, give me Consumption and take these sticky dreams away from me."

MELCHIOR: With any luck, he'll ignore *that* prayer.

MORITZ: Melchi, I can't focus—on *anything*. Even now, it seems like... Well, I see, and hear, and feel, quite clearly. And yet, everything seems so strange...

MELCHIOR: But all those illustrations I gave you—didn't they help illuminate your dreams?

MORITZ: They only multiplied everything ten times! Instead of merely seeing Stockings, now I'm plagued by Labia Majora and—

(Frau Gabor enters with tea.)

FRAU GABOR: Well, here we are, with tea. Herr Stiefel, how are you?

MORITZ: Very well, thank you, Frau Gabor.

FRAU GABOR *(Skeptical)*: Yes?

MELCHIOR *(Busting him)*: Just think, Mama. Moritz was up, reading all through the night.

MORITZ: Uh, conjugating Greek.

FRAU GABOR: You must take care of yourself, Moritz. Surely, your health is more important than Ancient Greek.

(Indicating his books) Now, what have *you* been reading, Melchior?

MELCHIOR: Goethe's *Faust*, actually.

FRAU GABOR: Really? At your age?...

MELCHIOR: It's so beautiful, Mama.

MORITZ *("Indeed")*: So haunting.

FRAU GABOR: Still, I should have thought...

But surely, you boys are now of an age to decide for yourselves what is good for you and what is not. *(Sighs)* If you need anything else, children, call me.

(Frau Gabor goes out.)

MORITZ: Well, your mother certainly is remarkable.

MELCHIOR *("Yes, but")*: Until she catches her son reading Goethe.

MORITZ: I think she meant the story of Gretchen and her illegitimate child.

MELCHIOR: Yes. You see how obsessively everyone fixes on that story. It's as if the entire world were mesmerized by penis and vagina.

MORITZ: Well, *I* am. All the more so, I'm afraid, since reading your essay. What you wrote about the... *female*... I can't stop thinking about it. *(Pulls out the essay)* This part here—is it true?

MELCHIOR: Absolutely.

MORITZ: But, how can *you* understand that, Melchi? What the *woman* must feel.

MELCHIOR *("Why not?")*: Giving yourself over to someone else?... Defending yourself until, finally, you surrender and feel Heaven break over you?...

(Moritz nods.)

I just put myself in her place—and imagine...

MORITZ *("You've got to be kidding")*: Really?! *(Flipping through the essay—one diagram after another—increasingly mesmerized)* What it feels like?... for the *woman*?...

(A twelve-string guitar sounds—subtle chords, a world of longing. The Boys and Girls gather around Melchior and Moritz in radiant light, singing and moving as a chorus. The Boys hold copies of Melchior's essay.)

MELCHIOR:

Where I go, when I go there,
No more memory anymore—
Only drifting on some ship;
The wind that whispers, of the distance, to shore...

MORITZ:

Where I go, when I go there,
No more listening anymore—
Only hymns upon your lips;
A mystic wisdom, rising with them, to shore...

ERNST:

Touch me—just like that.
And that—O, yeah—now, that's heaven.
Now, that I like.
God, that's so nice.
Now lower down, where the figs lie...

(Melchior turns back to Moritz. The lights shift back to the lamplit study, but the Boys and Girls hover, singing quietly, underscoring the scene.)

MORITZ *(Still in his private moment with the diagrams)*:... Still, you must admit... with all the differing... *(Mispronouncing, with a "hard g")* geni... geni...

MELCHIOR *(Correcting his pronunciation)*: Genitalia?

MORITZ: Genitalia. It truly *is* daunting—I mean, how... everything might...

MELCHIOR: Measure up?

(Moritz looks stricken.)

Fit?

(More stricken.)

Moritz, not that I'm saying I *myself* have ever—
MORITZ: Not that *I'm* saying I wouldn't want... Would ever want to *not*— Would ever *not* want...
MELCHIOR: Moritz?
MORITZ: I have to go!

(Moritz abruptly rushes out.)

MELCHIOR: Moritz, wait—

(But he's gone.)

(More to himself) Moritz...

(Frau Gabor enters, and clears the tea.)

FRAU GABOR: Melchior, what is it?
MELCHIOR: Nothing, Mama.
FRAU GABOR: Has Moritz gone?
MELCHIOR: Yes.
FRAU GABOR: Well, he does look awfully pale, don't you think? I wonder, is that *Faust* really the best thing for him?

(Frau Gabor exits. Melchior shakes his head, incredulous. The world recedes. All reenter the song.)

OTTO:

> *Where I go, when I go there,*
> *No more shadows anymore—*
> *Only you there in the kiss;*
> *And nothing missing, as you're drifting, to shore...*

GEORG:

> *Where I go, when I go there,*
> *No more weeping anymore—*
> *Only in and out your lips;*
> *The broken wishes, washing with them, to shore...*

MELCHIOR AND MORITZ:
>*Touch me—all silent.*
>*Tell me—please—all is forgiven.*
>*Consume my wine.*
>*Consume my mind.*
>*I'll tell you how, how the winds sigh...*

BOYS AND GIRLS:
>*Touch me—*

GEORG:
>*—just try it.*
>*Now, there—that's it—God, that's heaven.*
>*I'll love your light.*
>*I'll love you right...*
>*We'll wander down where the sins cry...*

BOYS AND GIRLS:
>*Touch me—just like that.*
>*Now lower down, where the sins lie...*
>
>*Love me—just for a bit...*
>*We'll wander down, where the winds sigh...*
>
>*Where the winds sigh...*
>*Where the winds sigh...*

SCENE 5

Afternoon. Melchior and Wendla discover each other in the woods.

WENDLA: Melchior Gabor?

MELCHIOR (*In disbelief*): Wendla Bergman?! Like a tree-nymph fallen from the branches. What are you doing—alone up here?

WENDLA: Mama's making May wine. I thought I'd surprise her with some woodruff. And you?

MELCHIOR: This is my favorite spot. My private place—for thinking.

WENDLA *(Starts away)*: Oh. I'm sorry—

MELCHIOR: No—no. Please.

(She pauses.)

So… how have you been doing?

WENDLA: Well, this morning was wonderful. Our youth group brought baskets of food and clothing to the day-laborers' children.

MELCHIOR: I remember when we used to do that. Together.

WENDLA: You should have seen their faces, Melchior. How much we brightened their day.

MELCHIOR: Actually, it's something I've been thinking a lot about.

WENDLA: The day-laborers?

MELCHIOR *("No")*: Our little acts of charity. What do you think, Wendla, can our Sunday School deeds really make a difference?

WENDLA: They have to. Of course. What other hope do those people have?

MELCHIOR: I don't know, exactly. But I fear that Industry is fast determining itself firmly against them.

WENDLA: Against us all, then.

MELCHIOR: Thank you, yes!

WENDLA: It seems to me: what serves *each* of us best is what serves *all* of us best.

MELCHIOR: Indeed.

(A beat.)

Wendla Bergman, I have known you all these years, and we've never truly talked.

WENDLA: We have so few opportunities. Now that we're older.

MELCHIOR: True. In a more progressive world, of course, we could all attend the same school. Boys and girls together. Wouldn't that be remarkable?

(In the moment of intellectual engagement, Melchior has drawn so close to Wendla that she grows self-conscious and pulls back.)

WENDLA: What time is it?

MELCHIOR: Must be close to four.

WENDLA: Oh? I thought it was later. I paused and lay so long in the moss by the stream, and just let myself dream... I thought it must be... later.

MELCHIOR: Then, can't you sit for a moment? When you lean back against this oak, and stare up at the clouds, you start to think hypnotic things...

WENDLA: I have to be back before five.

MELCHIOR: But, when you lie here, such a strange, wonderful peace settles over you...

WENDLA: Well, for a moment maybe.

(Wendla and Melchior settle beneath the oak. The lights shift, isolating them in a world of vibrant shadow. A classic arpeggio begins.)

Just too unreal, all this.
Watching the words fall from my lips...

MELCHIOR:
Baiting some girl—with hypotheses!

WENDLA AND MELCHIOR:
Haven't you heard the word of your body?

(Melchior reaches, tentatively, takes Wendla's hand. They begin a private pas de deux.)

MELCHIOR:
Don't feel a thing—you wish.

WENDLA:
Grasping at pearls with my fingertips...

MELCHIOR:
> *Holding her hand like some little tease.*

WENDLA AND MELCHIOR:
> *Haven't you heard the word of my wanting?*

> *O, I'm gonna be wounded.*
> *O, I'm gonna be your wound.*
> *O, I'm gonna bruise you.*
> *O, you're gonna be my bruise.*

> *Just too unreal, all this.*

WENDLA:
> *Watching his world slip through my fist...*

MELCHIOR:
> *Playing with her in your fantasies.*

WENDLA AND MELCHIOR:
> *Haven't you heard a word—how I want you?*

> *O, I'm gonna be wounded.*
> *O, I'm gonna be your wound.*
> *O, I'm gonna bruise you.*
> *O, you're gonna be my bruise.*

(The lights shift. Back to the woods.)

WENDLA: The sun's setting, Melchior. Truly, I'd better go.
MELCHIOR *(Touches her)*: We'll go together. I'll have you on
the bridge in ten minutes.

*(She hesitates, then allows him to take her hand. They walk
off together.)*

SCENE 6

The schoolyard. Georg, Hanschen, Ernst and Otto wait expectantly.

OTTO *(Pointing)*: Look—there he is!

(Moritz bounds on.)

HANSCHEN: So, did you get caught?
MORITZ: No—no—thank God—
ERNST: But, you're trembling.
MORITZ: For joy. For pure and certain joy!
GEORG *(Sarcastic)*: Cross your heart?
MORITZ: Twice over!

(Melchior enters.)

ERNST: Melchior!
MELCHIOR: Moritz, I've been looking for you.
GEORG: He snuck into the headmaster's office.
MELCHIOR: Moritz, what were you thinking?
MORITZ: I had to, Melchi. I just had to.
    The good news is: I *passed*!
HANSCHEN: The middle-terms, that is.
MORITZ: Yes. Everything will now be determined by the final exams. Still, I know I passed. Truly, Heaven must feel like this.

(Melchior embraces Moritz. The lights shift.
    Headmaster Knochenbruch is revealed, as if in his office. He turns to Fraulein Knuppeldick.)

HERR KNOCHENBRUCH: Well, well. Fraulein Knuppeldick.
FRAULEIN KNUPPELDICK: Herr Knochenbruch?
HERR KNOCHENBRUCH: Now that... that skittish, near-aphasic moron...
FRAULEIN KNUPPELDICK: Moritz Stiefel.

HERR KNOCHENBRUCH *("Indeed")*: Has somehow passed our middle-term exams, it would appear we face a certain dilemma.

FRAULEIN KNUPPELDICK: Ah.

HERR KNOCHENBRUCH: The upper grade, as we know, will hold only sixty. I hardly think we can promote sixty-one.

FRAULEIN KNUPPELDICK: Hardly, Herr Knochenbruch. But, let us look to the finals ahead.

HERR KNOCHENBRUCH: Yes?...

FRAULEIN KNUPPELDICK: Remember, it is I who shall be marking *them*.

HERR KNOCHENBRUCH: Then *I* am assured the good name of our school is secure.

(Herr Knochenbruch and Fraulein Knuppeldick exchange a look.)

SCENE 7

Afternoon. A windy day. Wendla, Martha, Thea and Anna walk arm in arm.

ANNA: Shall we take the short way home?

THEA: No no—by the bridge.

WENDLA: After two hours marching with that medicine ball?!

THEA: Come on!

ANNA *(Teasing)*: Someone wants to see: has Melchi Gabor taken a raft out?

THEA *("Even so")*: Last one there has to hold hands with Hanschen!...

(The Girls start off.)

ANNA: Martha, careful—your braid's coming loose.

MARTHA *(Concerned)*: No.

THEA: Just let it. Isn't it a nuisance for you—day and night. You may not cut it short, you may not wear it down...

WENDLA: Tomorrow, I'm bringing scissors.

MARTHA: For God's sake, Wendla, no! Papa beats me enough
    as it is.
WENDLA: Really?
MARTHA: No, no, I— It's nothing.
THEA: Martha...?
ANNA: Martha, we're your friends...

    (A beat.)

MARTHA: Well, when I don't do as he likes...
ANNA: What?
MARTHA: Some nights... Papa yanks out his belt.
THEA: But where is your mama?
MARTHA: "We have rules in this house. Your father will not
    be disobeyed."

    (A beat.)

    The other night, I ran for the door. "Out the door? All
    right, I like that. That's where you'll spend the night—
    out on the street."
THEA: No!
MARTHA: It was so cold.
ANNA: My God.

    (A beat.)

WENDLA: He beats you with a belt?
MARTHA: Anything.
WENDLA: With a buckle?
MARTHA *(Rolls up her sleeve)*: Right there...
ANNA: Oh my God!
WENDLA: Martha, the welts—they're terrible.
ANNA: We must tell someone.
MARTHA: Anna, no!
ANNA: But we must.
MARTHA: No, no, please. They'd throw me out for good.
THEA: Like what happened to Ilse, you mean.
WENDLA: Remember!

ANNA: But still...

MARTHA: Anna, no.

>*(The utter degradation)* Just look what's become of Ilse now! Living who knows where—with who knows *who*?!

WENDLA: I just wish I could somehow go through it for you...

(A beat.)

THEA: My Uncle Klaus says, "If you don't discipline a child, you don't love it."

MARTHA: That must be.

(A beat.)

ANNA: When I have children, I'll let them be free. And they'll grow strong and tall.

THEA: Free? But how will we know what to do if our parents don't tell us?

(A menacing eighth-note guitar riff. The lights shift. We enter the song world of Martha. Her mother, Frau Bessell, casting a long shadow.

>*Over the course of the first verses, Wendla, Anna and Thea walk off, one after the other.)*

FRAU BESSELL: Martha, time for bed now.

MARTHA:

>*There is a part I can't tell*
>*About the dark I know well...*

FRAU BESSELL: Martha, darling...?

(No response.)

Put on that new nightgown. The pretty ruffled one your father bought you.

MARTHA:

> *You say, "Time for bed now, child,"*
> *Mom just smiles that smile—*
> *Just like she never saw me.*
> *Just like she never saw me...*
>
> *So, I leave, wantin' just to hide.*
> *Knowin' deep inside*
> *You are comin' to me.*
> *You are comin' to me...*
>
> *You say all you want is just a kiss good night,*
> *Then you hold me and you whisper, "Child, the Lord*
>   *won't mind.*
> *It's just you and me.*
> *Child, you're a beauty."*
>
> *"God, it's good—the lovin'—ain't it good tonight?*
> *You ain't seen nothin' yet—gonna treat you right.*
> *It's just you and me.*
> *Child, you're a beauty."*

(A knocking on a door. Ilse is revealed in song light. Her father, Herr Neumann, peers out of the dark.)

HERR NEUMANN: Ilse...? Ilse. Story time.

ILSE:

> *I don't scream. Though I know it's wrong.*
> *I just play along.*
> *I lie there and breathe.*
> *Lie there and breathe...*
>
> *I wanna be strong—*
> *I want the world to find out*
> *That you're dreamin' on me,*
> *Me and my "beauty."*

ILSE AND MARTHA:
> *Me and my "beauty"...*

ILSE, MARTHA AND BOYS:
> *You say all you want is just a kiss good night,*
> *Then you hold me and you whisper, "Child, the Lord*
>   *won't mind.*
> *It's just you and me.*
> *Child, you're a beauty."*
>
> *"God, it's good—the lovin'—ain't it good tonight?*
> *You ain't seen nothin' yet—gonna teach you right.*
> *It's just you and me.*
> *Child, you're a beauty."*
>
> *There is a part I can't tell*
> *About the dark I know well.*
>
> *There is a part I can't tell*
> *About the dark I know well.*
>
> *There is a part I can't tell*
> *About the dark I know well.*
>
> *There is a part I can't tell*
> *About the dark I know well...*

(Blackout.)

SCENE 8

The woods. Melchior sits, writing in his journal.

MELCHIOR *(Reading aloud as he writes)*: 27 November. The
trouble is: the terrible prerogative of the... Parentocracy
in Secondary Education...

*(The lights shift, rising on Moritz in the schoolyard. Herr
Knochenbruch and Fraulein Knuppeldick summon him.)*

FRAULEIN KNUPPELDICK: Herr Stiefel, may we have a word with you?

(Moritz stiffens.)

MELCHIOR *(Continuing in his journal):...* a world where teachers—like parents—view us as merely so much raw material for an obedient and productive society...

(Herr Knochenbruch and Fraulein Knuppeldick approach Moritz, and address him in private conference.)

. . . a unified, military-like body, where all that is weak must be hammered away...

(Herr Knochenbruch and Fraulein Knuppeldick continue on their way, leaving Moritz looking like a ghost.)

. . . where the progress of the students reflects back only on the rank and order of the faculty, and therefore a single low mark can be seen as a threat to—

(Moritz wanders off—lost. Wendla approaches Melchior.)

WENDLA: Melchior?
MELCHIOR *(Jumps up, startled)*: You?!...
WENDLA *(Shrugs)*: I was lying by the stream, and then... I saw you here...
MELCHIOR: Yes.

(An awkward pause.)

WENDLA: So...
MELCHIOR: So... the stream. Dreaming again?...
WENDLA: I was, I guess.
MELCHIOR: And, what were you dreaming of?
WENDLA: It's silly.
MELCHIOR: Tell me.

WENDLA: I dreamed I was a clumsy little girl, who spilt my father's coffee. And when he saw what I had done, he yanked out his belt and whipped me.

MELCHIOR: Wendla, that kind of thing doesn't happen anymore. Only in stories.

WENDLA: Martha Bessell is beaten almost every evening—the next day, you can see the welts. It's terrible.

Really, it makes you boiling hot to hear her tell it. Lately, I can't think about anything else.

MELCHIOR: Someone should file a complaint.

WENDLA: You know... I've never been beaten. Not once. I can't even imagine it. It must be just awful.

MELCHIOR: I don't believe anyone is ever better for it.

WENDLA: I've tried hitting myself—to find out how it feels, really, *inside*.

(Wendla sees a switch on the ground and picks it up.)

With this switch, for example? It's tough. And thin.

(She offers Melchior the switch. He takes it. Tries it, through the air.)

MELCHIOR: It'd draw blood.

WENDLA: You mean, if *you* beat me with it?...

MELCHIOR: Beat you?

WENDLA: Me.

MELCHIOR: Wendla, what are you thinking?!

WENDLA: Nothing.

MELCHIOR: I could never beat you.

WENDLA: But if I let you?

MELCHIOR: Never.

WENDLA: But if I asked you to?

MELCHIOR: Have you lost your mind?

WENDLA: Martha Bessell, she told me—

MELCHIOR: Wendla! You can't envy someone being beaten.

WENDLA: But I've never been beaten—my entire life. I've never... felt...

MELCHIOR: What?

WENDLA: *Anything.*

(No response.)

Please. Melchior...

(She offers him her backside. He considers, then strikes her lightly.)

I don't feel it!
MELCHIOR: Maybe not, with your dress on.

(Wendla hikes her skirt, offering Melchior the prospect of her somewhat more exposed backside.)

WENDLA: On my legs, then.
MELCHIOR: Wendla!
WENDLA: Come on. *Please.*
MELCHIOR: I'll teach you to say: "Please"...

(He firmly takes her by the arm, and strikes her with the switch.)

WENDLA *(Winces from the pain, but...)*: You're barely stroking me.

(He strikes her again.)

MELCHIOR: How's that then?
WENDLA: Martha's father, he uses his belt. He draws blood, Melchi.

(Melchior strikes her again.)

MELCHIOR: How's that?
WENDLA *(A lie)*: Nothing.
MELCHIOR: And that?
WENDLA: *Nothing.*
MELCHIOR: You bitch. I'll beat the hell out of you.

(Melchior flings the switch aside and throws Wendla to the ground, so violently that she begins sobbing.

Suddenly, he realizes what he's done. He stumbles, sobbing, into the woods. Otto and Georg are revealed, soulful members of the band.)

OTTO *(Gently)*:
> *O, you're gonna be wounded.*
> *O, I'm gonna be your wound...*

OTTO AND GEORG:
> *O, I'm gonna bruise you.*
> *O, you're gonna be my bruise...*

SCENE 9

The Stiefel sitting room. Moritz approaches his father, Herr Stiefel.

MORITZ: Father...?
HERR STIEFEL: Moritz.

> *(Moritz remains silent.)*

Yes...?
MORITZ: Well, I, uh, was wondering—hypothetically speaking—what would happen if...
HERR STIEFEL: "If..."?
MORITZ: If, one day, I, uh, failed. Not that—
HERR STIEFEL: You're telling me you've failed?
MORITZ: No—no! I only meant—
HERR STIEFEL: You've failed, haven't you? I can see it on your face.
MORITZ: Father, no!

> *(Herr Stiefel strikes Moritz.)*

Father—!

(Herr Stiefel strikes Moritz again. And again. He turns away in disgust.)

HERR STIEFEL: Well, it's finally come to this. I can't say I'm surprised.

(A beat.)

Failed.

(A beat.)

So, now, what are your mother and I supposed to do?

(No response.)

You tell me, Son. What?

(No response.)

How can she show her face at the Missionary Society?

(No response.)

What do I tell them at the Bank?

(No response.)

How do we go to Church?

(No response.)

What do we say?

(No response.)

My son. Failed.

(A beat.)

Failed.

(A beat.)

Thank God my father never lived to see this day.

(The lights fade, and simultaneously rise on...)

SCENE 10

Two discrete spaces are revealed. Over the course of the scene, the lights shift back and forth between them.

Frau Gabor sits, as if in her study, writing a letter.

Moritz steps forward, on the other side of the stage—in brilliant concert light—reading that letter.

A driving beat underscores the scene, building as Moritz sings.

FRAU GABOR: Dear Herr Stiefel—

(Thinks again) Moritz, I've spent the entire day thinking about your note. Truly, it touched me, it did, that you'd think of me as a friend. Of course, I was saddened to hear that your exams came off rather less well than you'd hoped, and that you will not be promoted, come fall.

And yet, I must say straightaway, that fleeing to America is hardly the solution. And even if it were, I cannot provide the money you request.

MORITZ:

Uh-huh... uh-huh... uh-huh... well, fine.
Not like it's even worth the time.
But still, you know, you wanted more.
Sorry, it won't change—been there before.

FRAU GABOR: You would do me wrong, Herr Stiefel, to read into my refusal any lack of affection. On the contrary, as Melchior's mother, I truly believe it to be my duty (to curb this momentary loss of)—

MORITZ:

> *The thing that sucks—okay?—for me,*
> *A thousand bucks, I'm, like, scot-free.*
> *And I mean, please... That's all I need.*
> *Get real—okay? By now, you know the score.*

FRAU GABOR: Should you like, I am ready to write to your parents. I will try to convince them that no one could have worked harder last semester, and also that too rigorous a condemnation of your current misfortune (could have the gravest possible effect on)—

MORITZ:

> *You wanna laugh. It's too absurd.*
> *You start to ask. Can't hear a word.*
> *You wanna crash and burn. Right, tell me more.*

FRAU GABOR: Still, Herr Stiefel, one thing in your letter disturbed me. Your—what shall we call it?—veiled threat that, should escape not be possible, you would take your own life.

MORITZ:

> *Okay so, now we do the play.*
> *Act like we so care. No way.*
> *You'll write my folks? Well, okay. Babe, that's how it goes.*

FRAU GABOR: My dear boy, the world is filled with men—businessmen, scientists, scholars even—who have done rather poorly in school, and yet gone on to brilliant careers. Consider, for example, that rare and estimable essayist, Leopold Habebald—

MORITZ:

> *They're not my home. Not anymore.*
> *Not like they so were before.*
> *Still, I'll split, and they'll, like... Well, who knows?*
> *Who knows? Who knows?*

FRAU GABOR: In any case, I assure you that your present misfortune will have no effect on my feelings for you, or on your relationship with Melchior.

(The Boys stride forward, one after the other, and join Moritz—a rousing punk-rock anthem.)

MORITZ AND HANSCHEN:
> *Uh-huh... uh-huh... uh-huh... well, fine.*
> *Not like it's even worth the time.*
> *But still, you know, you wanted more.*

HANSCHEN:
> *Okay, so nothing's changed.*

MORITZ:
> *Heard that before.*

MORITZ AND OTTO:
> *You wanna laugh. It's too absurd.*
> *You start to ask. Can't hear a word.*

OTTO:
> *You're gonna crash and burn.*

MORITZ:
> *Right, tell me more.*

MORITZ AND ERNST:
> *You start to cave. You start to cry.*
> *You try to run. Nowhere to hide.*

GEORG:
> *You want to crumble up, and close that door.*

FRAU GABOR: So, head high, Herr Stiefel. And do let me hear from you soon. In the meantime, I am unchangingly and most fondly yours, Fanny Gabor.

(Lights out on Frau Gabor. Moritz commands his post-punk space.)

MORITZ:

> *Just fuck it—right? Enough. That's it.*
> *You'll still go on. Well, for a bit.*
> *Another day of utter shit—*
> *And then there were none.*

MORITZ AND OTTO:

> *And then there were none...*

MORITZ, OTTO AND GEORG:

> *And then there were none...*

MORITZ AND BOYS:

> *And then there were none...*

> *(Moritz withdraws a gun from his vest pocket and strides off.)*

SCENE 11

A minimalist electronica motif sounds. Melchior is revealed in a haunted world of song. Distraught. Unable to shake the thought of what he's done to Wendla. He hounds his body with his hands. The Boys look on, and join as a chorus.

BOYS:

> *Flip on a switch, and everything's fine—*
> *No more lips, no more tongue, no more ears, no more eyes.*
> *The naked blue angel, who peers through the blinds,*
> *Disappears in the gloom of the mirror blue night.*

MELCHIOR:

> *But there's nowhere to hide from these bones, from my mind.*
> *It's broken inside—I'm a man and a child.*
> *I'm at home with a ghost, who got left in the cold.*
> *I'm locked out of peace, with no keys to my soul.*

BOYS:

> And the whispers of fear, the chill up the spine,
> Will steal away too, with a flick of the light.
> The minute you do, with fingers so blind,
> You remove every bit of the blue from your mind.

MELCHIOR AND BOYS:

> But there's nowhere to hide, from the ghost in my mind,
> It's cold in these bones—of a man and a child.
> And there's no one who knows, and there's nowhere to go.
> There's no one to see who can see to my soul...

(Wendla enters, holding Melchior's journal. The lights shift abruptly—from a cool "mirror blue" to the warm light of dusk—revealing Melchior in a hayloft.)

WENDLA: So, here you are.

MELCHIOR: Go away. Please.

WENDLA: There's a storm coming, you know. You can't sit sulking in some hayloft.

MELCHIOR: Out.

(A beat.)

WENDLA: Everyone's at Church. Rehearsing for our Michaelmas chorale. I slipped out.

MELCHIOR: Yes. Well.

(A beat.)

WENDLA: Your friend Moritz Stiefel is absent. Someone said he's been missing all day.

MELCHIOR: I expect he's had his fill of Michaelmas.

WENDLA: Perhaps.

(A beat.)

You know, I have your journal.

MELCHIOR: You do?!

WENDLA: You left it. The other day. I confess, I tried reading part of it—

MELCHIOR: Just leave it. Please.

(Wendla climbs into the hayloft, sets down the journal.)

WENDLA: Melchior, I'm sorry about... what happened. Truly, I am. I understand why you'd be angry at me. I don't know *what* I was thinking—

MELCHIOR: Don't.

WENDLA: But how can I not—

MELCHIOR: Please. Please. Don't.

(A beat.)

We were confused. We were both just...

WENDLA: But it was my fault that—

MELCHIOR: Don't—please—*no*! It was me—all me. Something in me started, when I hit you.

WENDLA: Something in *me*, too.

MELCHIOR: But I hurt you—

WENDLA: Yes, but still—

MELCHIOR: No more! My God. No more. Just—*please*.

(A beat.)

You should go.

(A beat. Wendla kneels beside Melchior.)

WENDLA: Won't you come out to the meadow now, Melchior? It's dark in here, and stuffy. We can run through the rain—get soaked to the skin—and not even care.

MELCHIOR: Forgive me...

WENDLA: It was *me*. All me.

(Wendla cradles his head on her breast.)

MELCHIOR: I can hear your heart beat, Wendla.

(Melchior reaches to kiss Wendla.)

WENDLA: Oh Melchi—
    (Then, hesitating) I don't know.
MELCHIOR *(Cradling her head on his breast)*: No matter where I
    am, I hear it, beating...
WENDLA: And I hear yours.

(Melchior leans close, kisses Wendla.)

Melchior...

(He kisses her again. Presses his body onto hers.)

No—wait—no—
MELCHIOR: Wendla...
WENDLA: Wait—stop. I can't. We're not supposed to.
MELCHIOR: What?

(No response.)

Not supposed to what? Love? I don't know—is there such
a thing? I hear your heart...

*(Gospel-tinged music with a modern groove begins. The Boys
and Girls are revealed, gathered in quiet chorus.)*

... I feel you breathing—everywhere—the rain, the hay...
    Please. Please, Wendla.

(He presses himself forward. Kisses her.)

BOYS AND GIRLS *(Quietly)*:
    I believe,
    I believe,
    I believe,
    Oh I believe.
    All will be forgiven—I believe.

(The song continues under, growing in intensity, for the rest of the scene.)

WENDLA: Melchi, no—it just—it's...
MELCHIOR: *What?* Sinful?
WENDLA: No. I don't know...
MELCHIOR: Then, why? Because it's *good*?

(No response.)

Because it makes us "feel" something?

(Wendla considers, then suddenly reaches and pulls Melchior to her. She kisses him. He holds her, and gently helps her lie back.)

BOYS AND GIRLS:
    I believe,
    I believe,
    I believe,
    Oh I believe.
    All will be forgiven—I believe.

    I believe,
    I believe,
    Oh I believe.
    There is love in Heaven—I believe.

MELCHIOR: Don't be scared.

(Wendla hesitates, then nods. Melchior kisses her. Touches her breast.)

WENDLA: No.
MELCHIOR: Please—
WENDLA: Don't. It...
MELCHIOR: What?

(Wendla takes his hand, places it back on her breast.)

BOYS AND GIRLS:
> *I believe,*
> *I believe,*
> *Oh I believe.*
> *There is love in Heaven—I believe.*

> *I believe,*
> *I believe,*
> *I believe,*
> *Oh I believe.*
> *All will be forgiven—I believe.*

(Melchior starts to unbutton Wendla's dress. He gently reaches up her legs.)

WENDLA: Wait...
MELCHIOR: It's just me. *(Off her look; reassuring her)* It's just me.

BOYS AND GIRLS:
> *I believe,*
> *I believe,*
> *I believe,*
> *Oh I believe,*

> *There is love in Heaven.*
>> *All will be forgiven.*
> *There is love in Heaven.*
>> *All will be forgiven.*

> *I believe...*
>> *There is love in Heaven.*
> *I believe...*
>> *All will be forgiven.*
> *I believe...*
>> *There is love in Heaven.*
> *I believe...*
>> *All will be forgiven.*

I believe...
There is love in Heaven.
I believe...
All will be forgiven.

(Melchior reaches inside Wendla's undergarments, strokes her gently.)

WENDLA: Now, there—now, *that's...*
MELCHIOR: Yes...?
WENDLA: Yes.

(As the song continues, Melchior climbs on top of Wendla, lowers his pants.)

BOYS AND GIRLS:
I believe...
There is love in Heaven.

I believe...
All will be forgiven.

BOYS AND GIRLS:
I believe...
There is love in Heaven.
I believe...
All will be forgiven.
I believe...
There is love in Heaven.
I believe...
All will be forgiven.

Peace and joy be with them,
Harmony and wisdom...

OTHER GIRLS:

Peace and joy be with them...

Harmony and wisdom...

(Melchior penetrates Wendla.)

WENDLA: Melchior—*oh!*...

BOYS AND GIRLS:
    I believe...

    (The song ends. The lights fade. End of Act One.)

ACT TWO

SCENE 1

Dusk. Church. The same time, the same day as the close of Act One. Music underscores, as Father Kaulbach delivers his sermon.

FATHER KAULBACH *(Mid-sermon)*:... Let us then turn today, children, to an adage much loved of Martin Luther: "To God, to our parents, to our teachers, we can never render sufficient gratitude."

(The scene shifts, revealing Wendla and Melchior in the hayloft. They are once again in their moment of love-making, as Father Kaulbach continues:)

How well we know: these words may strike our modern ear as merely quaint. As dubious. As old. And yet, let us pose this question—each of us—within our dark heart: in what ways have we honored, or dishonored, our father and mother? In what ways have we strayed—in soul, in body—from all the wise instruction of our clergymen, our teachers?

(The light fades on Father Kaulbach.
  Melchior gently withdraws himself from Wendla.)

MELCHIOR: Are you all right, Wendla?

(A song begins—subtly sweeping electronic keyboards. Concert light finds Wendla. The lights shift between the world of cloudless song and the lovers' uncertain moment in the hay-loft. The Boys and Girls look on, and sing as a chorus.)

WENDLA:
> *Something's started crazy—*
> *Sweet and unknown.*
> *Something you keep*
> *In a box on the street—*
> *Now it's longing for a home...*

WENDLA, GIRLS AND BOYS:
> *And who can say what dreams are?...*

WENDLA:
> *Wake me in time to be lonely and sad.*

WENDLA, GIRLS AND BOYS:
> *And who can say what we are?...*

WENDLA:
> *This is the season for dreaming...*

> *And now our bodies are the guilty ones,*
> *Who touch,*
> *And color the hours;*

> *Night won't breathe*
> *Oh how we*
> *Fall in silence from the sky,*
> *And whisper some silver reply...*

MELCHIOR *(Still intent on his question)*: Wendla...?
WENDLA: I think so. Yes.

MELCHIOR:
> *Pulse is gone and racing—*
> *All fits and starts.*
> *Window by window,*
> *You try and look into*
> *This brave new you that you are.*

MELCHIOR, GIRLS AND BOYS:
> *And who can say what dreams are?...*

MELCHIOR:
> *Wake me in time to be out in the cold.*

MELCHIOR, GIRLS AND BOYS:
> *And who can say what we are?...*

MELCHIOR:
> *This is the reason for dreaming...*

MELCHIOR, WENDLA, GIRLS AND BOYS:
> *And now our bodies are the guilty ones—*
> *Our touch*
> *Will fill every hour.*

> *Huge and dark,*
> *Oh our hearts*
> *Will murmur the blues from on high,*
> *Then whisper some silver reply...*

GIRLS AND BOYS:
> *Wo-o-Wo-o-o*

(The Boys and Girls gather like an alt-rock choir around Melchoir and Wendla. Father Kaulbach is again revealed in church.)

FATHER KAULBACH: Ah, but children, children, in what ways have we cloaked, and hidden even from ourselves, the secret bargains we have made with our own devils...?

MELCHIOR, WENDLA, GIRLS AND BOYS:
> *And now our bodies are the guilty ones...*

(Moritz strides on, waving everyone away.)

MORITZ: Enough. Enough. *Enough.*

(The lights go electric, holding on Moritz.)

SCENE 2

Moritz looks out, as if he were the frontman in a garage band.

MORITZ:
> *Awful sweet to be a little butterfly.*
> *Just wingin' over things, and nothin' deep inside.*
> *Nothin' goin', goin' wild in you—you know—*
> *You're slowin' by the riverside or floatin' high and blue...*
>
> *Or, maybe, cool to be a little summer wind.*
> *Like, once through everything, and then away again.*
> *With a taste of dust in your mouth all day,*
> *But no need to know, like, sadness—you just sail away.*
>
> *'Cause, you know, I don't do sadness—not even a little bit.*
> *Just don't need it in my life—don't want any part of it.*
> *I don't do sadness. Hey, I've done my time.*
> *Lookin' back on it all—man, it blows my mind.*
>
> *I don't do sadness. So been there.*
> *Don't do sadness. Just don't care.*

(The song ends, and the lights shift. Twilight. A river. Moritz stands alone. He withdraws a gun from his pocket. Ilse suddenly enters. Sees him.)

ILSE: Moritz Stiefel!
MORITZ *(Frantically hiding the gun)*: Ilse?! You frightened me!

ILSE: Did you lose something?
MORITZ: Why did you frighten me?

(A beat.)

Damn it!
ILSE: What're you looking for?
MORITZ: If only I knew.
ILSE: Then what's the use of looking?

(A beat.)

MORITZ: So, where have you been keeping yourself?
ILSE: Priapia—the Artists' colony?
MORITZ: Yes.
ILSE: All those old buggers, Moritz. All so wild. So... Bohemian.
All they want to do is dress me up and paint me! That Johan Fehrendorf, he's a wicked one, actually. Always knocking easels down and chasing me. Dabbing me with his paintbrush. But then, that's men—if they can't stick you with one thing, they'll try another.

Oh God, Moritz, the other day we all got so drunk, I passed out in the snow—just lay there, unconscious, all night.

Then, I spent an entire week with Gustav Baum. *(Off his look)* Truly. Inhaling that ether of his! Until this morning, when he woke me with a gun, set against my breast. He said: "One twitch and it's the end." Really gave me the goosebumps.

But, how about you, Moritz—still in school?
MORITZ: Well, this semester I'm through.

(A beat.)

ILSE: God, you remember how we used to run back to my house and play pirates? Wendla Bergman, Melchior Gabor, you, and I...

(A plaintive guitar sounds. A spotlight finds Ilse.)

Spring and summer,
Every other day,
Blue wind gets so sad.
Blowin' through the thick corn,
Through the bales of hay,
Through the open books on the grass...

Spring and summer...

Sure, when it's autumn,
Wind always wants to
Creep up and haunt you—
Whistling, it's got you;
With its heartache, with its sorrow,
Winter wind sings, and it cries...

Spring and summer,
Every other day,
Blue wind gets so pained.

Blowin' through the thick corn,
Through the bales of hay,
Through the sudden drift of the rain...

Spring and summer...

(The lights shift—twilight resumes.)

MORITZ: Actually, I better go.
ILSE: Walk as far as my house with me.
MORITZ: And...?
ILSE: We'll dig up those old tomahawks and play together, Moritz—just like we used to.
MORITZ: We did have some remarkable times. Hiding in our wigwam...
ILSE: Yes. I'll brush your hair, and curl it, set you on my little hobby horse...
MORITZ: I wish I could.
ILSE: Then, why don't you?

MORITZ *(A lie)*: Eighty lines of Virgil, sixteen equations, a paper on the Hapsburgs...

(The world goes neon again.)

> *So, maybe I should be some kinda' laundry line—*
> *Hang their things on me, and I will swing 'em dry.*
> *You just wave in the sun through the afternoon,*
> *And then, see, they come to set you free, beneath the*
> *   risin' moon.*

MORITZ: ILSE:
   'Cause you know—

MORITZ	ILSE
I don't do sadness—not even a little bit.	*Spring and summer,*
	Every other day,
Just don't need it in my life—don't want any part of it.	*Blue wind gets so lost.*
	Blowin' through the thick corn,
I don't do sadness. Hey I've done my time.	*Through the bales of hay—*
Lookin' back on it all— man, it blows my mind.	*Spring and summer,*
	Every other day,
	Blue wind gets so lost.
I don't do sadness.	*Blowin' through the thick corn,*
	Through the bales of hay,
So been there.	*Through the wandering clouds of the dust...*
Don't do sadness.	
Just don't care.	*Spring and summer...*

(The concert light fades.)

MORITZ: Good night, Ilse.
ILSE: *Good night?*
MORITZ: Virgil, the equations—remember?
ILSE: Just for an hour.
MORITZ: I can't.

ILSE: Well, walk me at least.

MORITZ: Honestly, I wish I could.

ILSE: You know, by the time you finally wake up, I'll be lying on some trash heap.

(Ilse goes. Moritz winces.)

MORITZ: For the love of God, all I had to do was say yes.
(Calls after her) Ilse? Ilse...?

(He waits. If only he could run after her... But now, she's gone.)

So, what will I say? I'll tell them all, the angels, *I* got drunk in the snow, and sang, and played pirates... Yes, I'll tell them, I'm ready now. I'll *be* an angel.

(Moritz sighs, looks out on the night. He withdraws the gun from his pocket.)

Ten minutes ago, you could see the entire horizon. Now, only the dusk—the first few stars...
So dark. So dark. So dark...

(Moritz cocks the hammer of the gun. Sets the gun in his mouth. Blackout.)

SCENE 3

A cemetery in the pouring rain. Moritz's father, Herr Stiefel, stands, stoic, beside an open grave.

Frau Gabor approaches the grave to offer a flower. As she does, Melchior is revealed in song light. He begins to sing, giving voice to Herr Stiefel's inner thoughts.

One by one, the Boys and Girls step forward, dropping a flower on Moritz's grave, then continuing on their way, rejoining as a chorus.

MELCHIOR:

> *You fold his hands, and smooth his tie.*
> *You gently lift his chin—*
> *Were you really so blind, and unkind to him?*
>
> *Can't help the itch to touch, to kiss,*
> *To hold him once again.*
> *Now, to close his eyes, never open them?...*

MELCHIOR, BOYS AND GIRLS:

> *A shadow passed. A shadow passed,*
> *Yearning, yearning for the fool it called a home.*

MELCHIOR:

> *All things he never did are left behind;*
> *All the things his mama wished he'd bear in mind;*
> *And all his dad ever hoped he'd know.*
> *O-o-o-o-o-o—*
>
> *The talks you never had,*
> *The Saturdays you never spent,*
> *All the "grown-up" places you never went;*
>
> *And all of the crying you wouldn't understand,*
> *You just let him cry—"Make a man out of him."*

MELCHIOR, BOYS AND GIRLS:

> *A shadow passed. A shadow passed,*
> *Yearning, yearning for the fool it called a home.*

MELCHIOR:

> *All things he ever wished*
> *Are left behind;*
> *All the things his mama*
> *Did to make him mind;*
> *And how his dad*
> *Had hoped he'd grow.*
>
> *All things he ever lived*
> *Are left behind;*

> All the fears that ever
> Flickered through his mind;
> All the sadness that
> He'd come to own.
> O-o-o-o-o-o—

(Herr Stiefel moves to drop his flower, but hesitates. Melchior touches Herr Stiefel's chest, and the man abruptly collapses in grief, weeping over his son's grave.)

MELCHIOR, BOYS AND GIRLS:
> O-o-o-o-o-o...
>
> O-o-o-o-o-o...
>
> A shadow passed. A shadow passed,
> Yearning, yearning for the fool it called a home.

MELCHIOR:
> And, it whistles through the ghosts
> Still left behind...
> It whistles through the ghosts
> Still left behind...
> It whistles through the ghosts still left behind...
> O-o...

(Melchior drops the final flower.)

SCENE 4

The headmaster's office. Herr Knochenbruch summons Fraulein Knuppeldick.

HERR KNOCHENBRUCH: Fraulein Knuppeldick.
FRAULEIN KNUPPELDICK: Herr Knochenbruch...?
HERR KNOCHENBRUCH: We must take immediate and decisive steps, lest we be perceived as one of *those* institutions afflicted by the veritable epidemic of adolescent suicide.

FRAULEIN KNUPPELDICK: Indeed, sir. But, it will not be an easy war to win. There's not only the moral corruption of our youth, but the creeping sensuality of these liberal-minded times.

HERR KNOCHENBRUCH: I couldn't agree more. It's war. Naturally, there must be casualties.

(A beat.)

Bring the boy in.

FRAULEIN KNUPPELDICK: Certainly, Herr Knochenbruch.

(Fraulein Knuppeldick beckons Melchior in.)

HERR KNOCHENBRUCH: It would seem, young man, that all roads end in you. You do know what I mean?

MELCHIOR *("But, you don't understand…")*: I'm afraid—

HERR KNOCHENBRUCH *(Completing Melchior's sentence for him)*: As well one would be. Two days after his father learned of the young, uh…

FRAULEIN KNUPPELDICK *(Supplying the name)*: Moritz Stiefel…

HERR KNOCHENBRUCH:… Moritz Stiefel's death, he searched through the boy's effects and uncovered a certain depraved and atheistic document which made terribly clear—

FRAULEIN KNUPPELDICK: Terribly clear…

HERR KNOCHENBRUCH:… the utter moral corruption of the young man. A corruption which, no doubt, hastened the boy's end.

FRAULEIN KNUPPELDICK: Without question, Herr Knochenbruch.

HERR KNOCHENBRUCH: I am referring, as you may know, to a ten-page essay, entitled, coyly enough, "The Art of Sleeping With"… accompanied by—shall we say—life-like illustrations.

MELCHIOR: Herr Knochenbruch, if I could—

HERR KNOCHENBRUCH: Behave properly? Yes, that would be another affair entirely.

FRAULEIN KNUPPELDICK: Entirely.

HERR KNOCHENBRUCH: For our part, we have made a thorough examination of the handwriting of this obscene document, and compared it with that of every single pupil—

MELCHIOR: Sir, if you could show me only *one* obscenity—

HERR KNOCHENBRUCH: You must now answer *only* the precisely stated questions. With a swift and decisive "Yes" or "No."

(A beat.)

Melchior Gabor, did you write this?

(Herr Knochenbruch and Fraulein Knuppeldick turn and stare at Melchior. Music sounds—a dirty electric guitar chord, seemingly prompting a song. Herr Knochenbruch and Fraulein Knuppeldick exchange a look, then turn again and stare at Melchior. The guitar chord sounds again.)

FRAULEIN KNUPPELDICK: *Did you write this?*

(Herr Knochenbruch and Fraulein Knuppeldick turn and stare—awaiting an answer. The lights shift. A rocking beat kicks in. The Boys and Girls appear. Melchior turns out:)

MELCHIOR:

> *There's a moment you know... you're fucked—*
> *Not an inch more room to self-destruct.*
> *No more moves—oh yeah, the dead-end zone.*
> *Man, you just can't call your soul your own.*

OTTO:

> *But the thing that makes you really jump*
> *Is that the weirdest shit is still to come.*
> *You can ask yourself: hey, what have I done?*
> *You're just a fly—the little guys, they kill for fun.*

GEORG:

> *Man, you're fucked if you just freeze up,*
> *Can't do that thing—that keepin' still.*

HANSCHEN:
>   *But, you're fucked if you speak your mind,*

GEORG, OTTO AND HANSCHEN:
>   *And you know—uh-huh—you will.*

BOYS AND GIRLS:
>   *Yeah, you're fucked, all right—and all for spite.*
>   *You can kiss your sorry ass good-bye.*
>   *Totally fucked. Will they mess you up?*
>   *Well, you know they're gonna try.*

MELCHIOR *(Mocking the professors)*:
>   *Blaa blaa blaa blaa blaa blaa blaa...*

BOYS AND GIRLS:
>   *Blaa blaa blaa blaa blaa blaa blaa...*

>   *(The lights shift back: the headmaster's office. Herr Knochen-*
>   *bruch and Fraulein Knuppeldick again summon Melchior's*
>   *attention. Over the course of the next exchanges, the lights shift*
>   *back and forth—between the worlds of song and scene.)*

HERR KNOCHENBRUCH: Herr Gabor?

MELCHIOR:
>   *Disappear—yeah, well, you wanna try.*
>   *Wanna bundle up into some big-ass lie,*
>   *Long enough for them to all just quit.*
>   *Long enough for you to get out of it.*

HERR KNOCHENBRUCH: Herr Gabor, answer me.

MELCHIOR, BOYS AND GIRLS:
>   *Yeah, you're fucked, all right—and all for spite.*
>   *You can kiss your sorry ass good-bye.*
>   *Totally fucked. Will they mess you up?*
>   *Well, you know they're gonna try.*

HERR KNOCHENBRUCH: Melchior Gabor, for the last time...
HERR KNOCHENBRUCH AND FRAULEIN KNUPPELDICK: Did
    you write this?
MELCHIOR: Yes.

*(Herr Knochenbruch gestures, and Melchior is led away. The
lights go psychedelic.)*

MELCHIOR, BOYS AND GIRLS:
    Yeah, you're fucked all right—and all for spite.
    You can kiss your sorry ass good-bye.
    Totally fucked. Will they mess you up?
    Well, you know they're gonna try.

(And now even the grown-ups join the song:)

ALL:
    Blaa blaa blaa blaa blaa blaa blaa blaa
    Blaa blaa blaa blaa blaa,
    Blaa blaa blaa blaa blaa blaa blaa blaa
    Blaa blaa blaa blaa blaa...

    Blaa blaa blaa blaa blaa blaa blaa blaa
    Blaa blaa blaa blaa blaa,
    Blaa blaa blaa blaa blaa blaa blaa blaa
    Blaa blaa blaa blaa blaa...

    Totally fucked!

SCENE 5

*A vineyard at sunset. Church bells sounding in the distance.
Hanschen and Ernst loll in the grass.*

HANSCHEN: Those bells... So peaceful.
ERNST: I know. Sometimes, when it's quiet, in the evening
    like this, I imagine myself as a country pastor. With my

red-cheeked wife, my library, my degrees... Boys and girls, who live nearby, give me their hands when I go walking...

HANSCHEN: You can't be serious.

(A beat.)

Really, Ernst, you're such a sentimentalist! The pious, serene faces you see on the clergy, it's all an act—to hide their envy.

(Hanschen deftly scoots closer to Ernst.)

Trust me, there are only three ways a man can go. He can let the status quo defeat him—like Moritz. He can rock the boat—like Melchior—and be expelled. Or he can bide his time, and let the System work for *him*—like me.

(Hanschen scoots even closer to Ernst.)

Think of the future as a pail of whole milk. One man sweats and stirs—churning it into butter—like Otto, for example. Another man frets, and spills his milk, and cries all night. Like Georg. But, me, well, I'm like a pussycat, I just skim off the cream...

ERNST: Just skim off the cream?...

HANSCHEN: Right.

ERNST: But, what about the...?

    (Off Hanschen's look) You're laughing.

    What—?

    Hanschen?

(The lights shift. Hanschen leans into the spotlight and smoothly croons:)

HANSCHEN:

    Come, cream away the bliss,
    Travel the world within my lips,
    Fondle the pearl of your distant dreams...
    Haven't you heard the word of your body?

> *O, you're gonna be wounded.*
> *O, you're gonna be my wound.*
> *O, you're gonna bruise too.*
> *O, I'm gonna be your bruise...*

(The lights shift back. Hanschen leans over and kisses Ernst.)

ERNST: Oh God...

HANSCHEN: Mmm, I know. When we look back, thirty years from now, tonight will seem unbelievably beautiful.

ERNST: And, in the meantime...?

HANSCHEN: Why not?

(Hanschen kisses Ernst deeply.)

ERNST: On my way here this afternoon, I thought perhaps we'd only... talk.

HANSCHEN: So, are you sorry we—?

ERNST: Oh no—I love you, Hanschen. As I've never loved anyone.

HANSCHEN: And so you should.

(Hanschen shares the spotlight with Ernst.)

ERNST:

> *O, I'm gonna be wounded.*
> *O, I'm gonna be your wound.*

ERNST AND HANSCHEN:

> *O, I'm gonna bruise you.*
> *O, you're gonna be my bruise...*

(Wendla, Melchior, and the Boys and Girls appear in chorus. As the song continues, Ilse takes a letter from Melchior and delivers it to Wendla.)

ERNST, HANSCHEN, WENDLA, MELCHIOR, BOYS AND GIRLS:

> *O, you're gonna be wounded.*
> *O, you're gonna be my wound.*
> *O, you're gonna bruise too.*
> *O, I'm gonna be your bruise...*

SCENE 6

Wendla's bedroom. Wendla reads from Melchior's letter. Melchior is revealed, in a spotlight.

MELCHIOR *(From his letter)*: ". . . I have now seen, Wendla, how this contemptible bourgeois society works—how everything we touch is turned to dirt. In the end, we have only each other—we must build a different world. Despite what those whispering elders may say, I must set my head against your breast. We must let ourselves breathe and move again in that Paradise—"

(Doctor von Brausepulver and Frau Bergman enter. Wendla swiftly hides the letter in her sleeve. Doctor von Brausepulver attends her, pill bottle in hand. Frau Bergman hovers.)

DOCTOR VON BRAUSEPULVER: Now, now, don't fret. I've been prescribing these since before you were born, young lady. In fact, I recently recommended them to the utterly exhausted young Baroness von Witzelben. Eight days later—I'm pleased to report—she's off to a spa in Pyrmont, breakfasting on roast chicken and new potatoes.

(A beat.)

So, my child, three a day—an hour before meals. In a few weeks, you should be fine—breakfasting on suckling pig, no doubt.

FRAU BERGMAN: So, that's all it is, Doctor—anemia?

DOCTOR VON BRAUSEPULVER: C'est tout.

FRAU BERGMAN: And the nausea?

DOCTOR VON BRAUSEPULVER: Not uncommon.
     (Turns to Wendla) Trust me, child. You'll be fine.

(A beat.)

Frau Bergman, if I could have a word with you...?

FRAU BERGMAN: Certainly, Doctor.

(Frau Bergman leads Doctor von Brausepulver out. Wendla sits, quietly touches the letter in her sleeve.
In a moment, Frau Bergman reenters, and stares at her.)

WENDLA: Mama...?
FRAU BERGMAN: Wendla...? What have you done? To yourself? To me?

(No response.)

Wendla?
WENDLA: I, uh, don't know.
FRAU BERGMAN *(Not a question)*: You don't know.
WENDLA: Doctor von Brausepulver said I'm anemic.
FRAU BERGMAN: Well, probably. You're going to have a child.
WENDLA: A child?! But, I'm not married!
FRAU BERGMAN: Precisely.
        Wendla, what have you done?
WENDLA: I don't know. Truly, I don't.
FRAU BERGMAN: Oh, I think you know. And now I need his name.
WENDLA: His name? But what are you...
        (Abruptly realizing) That? How could that...? I just wanted to be with him...

WENDLA: ... To hold him and be close to him—	FRAU BERGMAN: Wendla, please. No more. You'll break my heart.

(A beat.)

WENDLA: My God, why didn't you tell me everything?

(Frau Bergman slaps Wendla.)

FRAU BERGMAN: Well, you are going to have to tell me who.

(No response.)

Wendla, I'm waiting.

(Wendla looks off into the distance.)

Georg Zirschnitz?

(No response.)

Then, who?

(No response.)

Hanschen Rilow?

(No response.)

Moritz Stiefel?

(No response.)

Melchior Gabor?

(Wendla quietly bursts into tears.)

Wendla, Melchior Gabor?

(No response.)

Wendla...?

(Wendla reluctantly hands Melchior's letter to her mother. As Frau Bergman opens it, Wendla stands, spotlit, like a singer in concert. She remains in this pool of light, her song playing in counterpoint to the following scenes:)

WENDLA:
> *Whispering...*
> *Hear the ghosts in the moonlight.*
> *Sorrow doing a new dance*
> *Through their bones, through their skin.*

Listening—
To the souls in the fool's night,
Fumbling mutely with their rude hands...
And there's heartache without end...

(The lights shift. Melchior's home. Melchior's father, Herr Gabor, addresses Frau Gabor:)

FRAU GABOR *(Mid-conversation)*: Hermann, this is our son.

HERR GABOR *(This is hard for him, too)*: For fifteen years, my darling, I have followed your lead, we have given the boy room. And now we must eat of the bitter fruit. He has shown himself utterly corrupt.

FRAU GABOR: He has not.

HERR GABOR: Hear me out.

FRAU GABOR: But I have. Melchior wrote an essay—every word of which was true. Are we so afraid of the truth we will join the ranks of cowards and fools? Twisting his naive act into evidence against him?

I will not have Melchior sent to some reformatory, pent up with degenerates and genuine criminals.

(Herr Gabor looks away, pained.)

WENDLA:

See the father bent in grief,
The mother dressed in mourning.
Sister crumples,
And the neighbors grumble.
The preacher issues warnings...

HERR GABOR: And now I must break your heart. *(Withdrawing a letter from his pocket)* This afternoon, Frau Bergman came to see me. Bearing a letter Melchior wrote to young Wendla, telling her he has no regret for what transpired in our hayloft...

FRAU GABOR: Impossible!

HERR GABOR: That he only longs to find again that bit of
    Paradise—
FRAU GABOR *(Reaching for the letter)*: Let me see that.
HERR GABOR: Yes, do have a look.

(Frau Gabor takes it, and is horrified by what she reads.)

WENDLA:

> *History...*
> *Little Miss didn't do right.*
> *Went and ruined all the true plans—*
> *Such a shame, such a sin.*
>
> *Mystery...*
> *Home alone on a school night.*
> *Harvest moon over the blue land;*
> *Summer longing on the wind...*

HERR GABOR: The wretched fact is: Melchior knew precisely
    what he was doing. And as that essay shows, he knew the
    danger of doing it. And yet, he went ahead. Defiling
    himself and all but destroying that girl.
    So, you tell me, Fanny—what shall we do?
FRAU GABOR: What you will.
    A reformatory.

*(Herr Gabor confronts Frau Gabor. She gazes into the distance,
stricken. The light on them fades.)*

WENDLA:

> *Had a sweetheart on his knees,*
> *So faithful and adoring.*
> *And he touched me,*
> *And I let him love me.*
> *So, let that be my story...*
>
> *Listening...*
> *For the hope, for the new life—*

Something beautiful, a new chance.
Hear, it's whispering, there, again...

SCENE 7

A Reformatory. In a darkened corner, Melchior opens a letter from Wendla.

MELCHIOR *(Reading from the letter)*: "My dear Melchior... I only pray this letter reaches you. I have written so many, and have heard nothing back. When I think of your life in that terrible place, my heart aches. If only I could be close to you, and talk to you—I have such remarkable news. Something has happened, Melchior. Something I can barely understand myself—"

(A group of Boys breaks in. Melchior quickly pockets the letter.)

DIETER: All right, each of you animals put in a coin.
RUPERT: Reinhold can put in for both of us.
REINHOLD: I beg your pardon!—
DIETER: All right, you, calm down. *(Means business)* Reinhold, cough it up.
REINHOLD *(Giving him a coin)*: Christ!
DIETER: Rupert, Ulbrecht—you, too.

(Dieter collects their coins, displays them, then sets them down in a pile.)

Now, whoever hits 'em, gets 'em.

(The Boys begin their circle jerk.)

ULBRECHT: Wait. *(To Melchior)* What are you lookin' at?
REINHOLD: Who?

(Melchior freezes.)

RUPERT: Gabor.

DIETER: He just wants a part of the sport.

MELCHIOR: No thank you.

RUPERT *(Ironic)*: Oh no, why would he dirty his hands?...

DIETER *("Right")*: Saving it for better things.

MELCHIOR: What do you mean?

ULBRECHT *(Ironic)*: Oh. A "good girl," wasn't she?

DIETER: Nobody taught the poor boy what parlor maids are for.

RUPERT: He was too busy fucking his slut—

MELCHIOR: You shit!

> *(Melchior lunges at Rupert. Rupert draws a straight razor, holds it to Melchior's throat.)*

RUPERT: Careful—razor burn.

MELCHIOR: Bastard!

DIETER *(Approaching)*: Check his pockets for money.

REINHOLD: Yes!

ULBRECHT *(Finds the letter in Melchior's pocket)*: Now what's this—a letter from his bitch?

MELCHIOR: Animals!

RUPERT *(Reading from the letter; with exaggerated prissiness)*: "My dear Melchior... I only pray this letter reaches you. I have written so many, and have heard nothing back..." *(Something in the text catches his eye)* Oooh, hang on, the perfect thing to grease the works. Listen up...

MELCHIOR: Son of a bitch!

> *(The scene shifts—a private garden. Frau Bergman greets Schmidt.)*

SCHMIDT: Frau Bergman?

FRAU BERGMAN: Thank you for meeting me. Your name was given me by a, uh, doctor friend. My daughter—

SCHMIDT: I understand. Now, listen to my instructions carefully. This Thursday, after nightfall, bring the girl to me. Gartenstrasse, Number Eleven. The door below the tavern. Knock three times—and three times only.

FRAU BERGMAN: But my *daughter*—! The procedure—is it *safe*?!

SCHMIDT *(Lifting a hand)*: We do what we can.

(The scene shifts back. The circle jerk is well underway.)

RUPERT *(Further on in the letter, as if he were reading from de Sade's journal)*: "…in my bed each night, I have so many dreams: of the better world that we will build, together with our child—"

MELCHIOR *(This is news to him)*: Child?!

RUPERT: You didn't know. *(To the Boys)* Put a pup in the bitch—and didn't even know.

DIETER: Forget the coins, we'll use "Mommy's" letter.

(Dieter tosses the letter into the center of their circle. The circle jerk intensifies.)

RUPERT *(Pushing Melchior's face down toward the floor)*: And *you* can lick it up!

(Melchior seizes the moment, wrests the razor from Rupert, and breaks free. Melchior brandishes the blade, fighting the Boys back.)

ULBRECHT: Get him!

REINHOLD: Grab him!

(Melchior leaps over the reformatory wall, the Boys in hot pursuit.

The scene shifts. Frau Bergman leads Wendla up a darkened street.)

WENDLA: But where are we going, Mama?

(Frau Bergman leads the girl to where Schmidt waits. Frau Bergman hands him some marks.)

SCHMIDT: Frau Bergman, good. I'll take her now.

(Frau Bergman pulls Wendla by the hand and gives her to Schmidt.)

WENDLA: Mama?!!
FRAU BERGMAN: I'll be there with you every moment.

(As Schmidt takes hold of Wendla, Frau Bergman lets her go. Schmidt leads Wendla off.)

WENDLA: Mama, don't leave me! *Mama???!!!*

(Frau Bergman looks around nervously, then bolts up the block.)

SCENE 8

The bridge. The Girls huddle around Ilse. She reaches into her dress, pulls out a letter from Melchior.

ILSE *(Reading from the letter)*: "...Ilse, I have been running for days, but at last I am back. Now, I beg you—for the sake of our old friendship. Bring Wendla to meet me tonight, in the graveyard behind the church..."
ANNA: Oh no...
ILSE: "...I will be waiting there at midnight... Melchior Gabor."

(Ilse looks up from the letter.)

THEA *(Sighs)*: So, he hasn't heard.
MARTHA: Waiting for Wendla...
THEA: Poor Melchior.
ANNA *(Correcting her)*: Poor *Wendla.*

SCENE 9

A graveyard. Moonlight. A sort of underworld in mist. Melchior enters, casts about.

MELCHIOR: Wendla...?!

(No response. Melchior sighs.)

Look at this—spend your life running from the Church, and where do you wind up?

(Melchior approaches a grave, kneels.)

Moritz, my old friend...

(A beat.)

Well, they won't get to me. Or Wendla. I won't—I won't let them. We'll build that world, together, for our child.

(Church bells chime: midnight. Melchior rises and looks about.)

Midnight.

(He listens for Wendla. Hears nothing. Sighs.)

My God, all these little tombs... And here—a fresh one... *(He pauses, reads the epitaph)* "Here Rests in God, Wendla Berg—"
   No?!
   (He bends closer, reads) "Born the... *Died*—"?! "Of anemia"??

(Melchior realizes, in numbed disbelief, what must have happened.)

Oh my God. Wendla, too?
   No. No. No...

(He doubles over, bereft. Spare piano chords—an otherworldly music begins.
Moritz appears—in song light—as if rising from his grave.)

MORITZ:
> *Those you've known,*
> *And lost, still walk behind you...*

MELCHIOR: Moritz?

MORITZ:
> *All alone,*
> *They linger till they find you...*

MELCHIOR: I've been a fool.

MORITZ:
> *Without them,*
> *The world grows dark around you—*
> *And nothing is the same until you know that they have*
> *   found you.*

(Melchior pulls out the straight razor.)

MELCHIOR: Well, you had the right idea. They'll scatter a little earth, and thank their God...

(As Melchior draws the razor to his throat, Wendla appears—in song light—as if rising from her grave.)

WENDLA:
> *Those you've pained*
> *May carry that still with them...*

(Melchior stops, stunned.)

MELCHIOR: Wendla?!

WENDLA:

> *All the same,*
> *They whisper: "All forgiven."*
>
> *Still, your heart says:*
> *The shadows bring the starlight,*
> *And everything you've ever been is still there in the dark*
> *night.*

MORITZ:

> *Though you know*
> *You've left them far behind—*
> *You walk on by yourself, and*
> *not with them,*
>
> *Still you know,*
> *They fill your heart and mind,*
> *When they say: "There's a way*
> *through this..."*

WENDLA:

> *When the northern*
> *wind blows,*
> *The sorrows*
> *Your heart holds,*
>
> *There are those who*
> *still know—*
> *They're still home;*
> *We're still home.*

(Melchior is tempted by his blade, but Moritz and Wendla gently intercede.)

MORITZ AND WENDLA:

> *Those you've known,*
> *And lost, still walk behind you.*
> *All alone,*
> *Their song still seems to find you.*
>
> *They call you,*
> *As if you knew their longing—*
>
> *They whistle through the lonely wind, the long blue*
> *shadows falling...*

(Melchior rises in the moonlight, resolved. He closes the razor.)

MELCHIOR:

> *All alone,*
> *But still I hear their yearning;*
> *Through the dark, the moon, alone there, burning.*

The stars, too,
They tell of spring returning—
And summer with another wind that no one yet has
  known...

They call me—
Through all things—
Night's falling,
But somehow on I go.

You watch me,
Just watch me—
I'm calling
From longing...

MORITZ:
  Still you know
  There's so much more to
    find—
  Another dream, another
    love you'll hold.

  Still you know
  To trust your own true mind
  On your way—you are not
    alone.

  There are those who still
    know—

WENDLA:
  When the northern wind
    blows,
  The sorrows
  Your heart's known—

  I believe...

(Melchior draws the ghosts of Wendla and Moritz to him, holds them.)

MELCHIOR:
  Now they'll walk on my arm through the distant night,
  And I won't let them stray from my heart.
  Through the wind, through the dark, through the winter
    light,
  I will read all their dreams to the stars.

MELCHIOR:

I'll walk now with them.

I'll call on their names,

*I'll see their thoughts
are known.*

*Not gone—
Not gone—
They walk with my heart—
I'll never let them go.*

I'll never let them go.

I'll never let them go...

*You watch me
Just watch me,
I'm calling.
I'm calling—
And one day all will know...*

MORITZ AND WENDLA
(Receding from Melchior):

Not gone.

Not gone.

Not gone.

(Melchior stands alone. The lights fade to black.)

SCENE 10

Coda

Ilse stands alone. A world washed in song light.

ILSE:

*Listen to what's in the heart of a child,
A song so big in one so small,
Soon you will hear where beauty lies—
You'll hear and you'll recall...*

The sadness, the doubt, all the loss, the grief,
Will belong to some play from the past;
As the child leads the way to a dream, a belief,
A time of hope through the land...

A summer's day,
A mother sings
A song of purple summer
Through the heart of everything.

(The Boys, the Girls, and the Adults enter, joining her in song.)

ALL:

And Heaven waits,
So close it seems
To show her child the wonders
Of a world beyond her dreams

The earth will wave with corn,
The days so wide, so warm,
And mares will neigh with
Stallions that they mate, foals they've borne...

And all shall know the wonder
Of purple summer...

And so, I wait.
The swallow brings
A song of what's to follow—
The glory of the spring.

The fences sway.
The porches swing.
The clouds begin to thunder,
Crickets wander, murmuring—

The earth will wave with corn,
The days so wide, so warm,
And mares will neigh with
Stallions that they mate, foals they've borne...

And all shall know the wonder—
I will sing the song
Of purple summer...

And all shall know the wonder—
I will sing the song
Of purple summer...

All shall know the wonder
Of purple summer...

THE END

AFTERWORD

I remember it so clearly: sitting on a bench in my back lawn in L.A., scratching out the Preface for the original edition of this book. Feeling so flush with what we'd achieved, through our "eight-year siege" to mount *Spring Awakening*, so full of hope that we could make some dent in the world.

I remember, just as clearly, deciding to begin the Preface with Wedekind's Masked Man. That notorious Symbolist figure who, at the conclusion of the groundbreaking original play, forcibly takes Melchior's hand and, breaking despair's hold on him, leads him from the graveyard—back to a world of culture and feeling, which the Man promises to open for him.

How ever could I have imagined that, fourteen years later, as I sit writing this Afterword, our own world would be full of masked men? And though our musical includes no Masked Man in its graveyard, in these Covid-pandemic days, in productions around the globe (if not in London), many a Melchior will look out on an audience in masks.

It was a real act of resistance, in 1891, when the original Masked Man, the angry young Frank Wedekind himself, first penned *Frühlings Erwachen*. To this day, it remains the most scabrous indictment ever written of adulthood. Of parents, teachers, and a clergy, so invested in their social prestige, they will sacrifice even their children to protect it.

More than a century later, in 1999, in the wake of the terrible shootings at Columbine, Duncan and I began work on our musical version. At the time, *Rent* was all the rage. And we were urged to follow its lead, to update the setting of our story to contemporary America—as Jonathan Larson had updated *La bohème*, and Laurents, Bernstein and Sondheim had done to *Romeo and Juliet*. Understandable as that impulse may have been, we resisted. I was wary of creating a period piece about teen struggles in the early 2000s. By leaving our tale firmly in nineteenth-century Bavaria and bringing a contemporary score to it, we aimed to create a more timeless fable, to hold up a more enduring mirror, one which could allow future generations of parents and children to see their own faces in its glass.

All these years later, I'm so thankful we did. For, despite all the continual shifts in our now-digital world, in the fifteen years since our Broadway premiere, the issues *Spring Awakening* raises (sadly) have not aged a whit. As I write this, broad-ranging abortion bans have gone into effect across the US. Youth suicide rates are rising at an alarming rate, world-wide, with teen mental health crises deemed a "pandemic within the pandemic." And in all the years since Columbine, there has been no significant change in gun-control laws in the States.

Indeed, 208 school shootings post-Columbine... In July 2017, six student survivors of the Parkland massacre performed in a local production of *Spring Awakening*. The premiere, which Duncan and I attended, seemed to transport me to the very origins of Western theatre, to the days of Ancient Greek Tragedies (which were themselves performed in masks). Like those ancient ceremonies, the production in Parkland felt like a cathartic rite; an act of communal cleansing; a collective mourning for the loss of seventeen friends "left behind."

From its inception, *Spring Awakening* has centered on the tragic ways we fail our children, by failing to listen to them. By remaining so stubbornly unwilling to hear what's in their hearts. It's hard to imagine that truth brought home more forcefully, or more exquisitely, than in the 2015/2016 revival by Deaf West Theatre. A revival in which all the words, whether spoken or sung, were simultaneously signed. In the Latin scene, for example, the Deaf and hard of hearing students were denied access to their language. They were not permitted to sign, but forced to vocalize. That muzzling force was felt in profound new ways, in the musical sequences as well. From the beginning, the songs in our show were intended to speak of what could not be said, with each song disclosing another "part I can't tell." If sign language was verboten, then each (signed) song became a further, illicit act of rebellion. In the musical numbers, the signing bloomed into choreography, with the effect that the words became the dance. The very words of those performers' bodies.

As noted in the Preface, as we crafted our show, we came to recognize that we did not need the Masked Man, because our contemporary score already played that role. The music and lyrics allowed our adolescent characters to give voice to their darker longings, to embrace that darkness as part of them, rather than as something to run from or repress. In our Deaf West revival, it was effectively the sign language which played the Masked Man.

Over the course of the pandemic, there have been multiple streamed productions of our musical, such as the one produced by London's Royal Central School of Speech and Drama. Each production I've seen, while remotely staged and virtually presented, has managed, still, to insist on the primacy of life-to-life connections. On our enduring need to touch and be touched. That need has felt all the more poignant, as the actors have not been permitted, in the staging, even to come near one another. In addition, many of those performers have been masked. And for me, it's been the masks themselves which have taken on the role of the Masked Man: allowing those formerly locked-up young performers to take the stage again, to rejoin their world. Beyond that, the masks have worked thematically for the piece, serving to remind us of our distance from one another, of the essential mystery of each other, of our need to ask consent from one another—if we are to take each other's hands.

After years of planning, our production at the Almeida was slated for spring and summer, 2020, and then twice postponed due to the closing of theatres. As the world reopens, it's all the more gratifying finally to be headed into rehearsal, and all the more intriguing to learn how all our lockdown months will inform the show. From the earliest days of *Spring Awakening* on Broadway, Rupert Goold has spoken to me of his own vision for the piece. Of a more inclusive production, which could feel thoroughly of the moment, underscoring the radicalism of young people today. (Young people thoroughly "woke"—or *awakened*.) Acknowledging, if tacitly, their newfound power and visibility in our post-social media world, as they march against injustice and refuse not to be heard. I have no doubt that Rupert's production will bring further honor to Wedekind's still-startling original play. And I'm truly grateful for the publication of this book to commemorate that.

S.S.
New York
October 2021

TESTIMONIALS

DUNCAN SHEIK (*composer, co-creator*)

When Steven Sater and I met one fateful day at a Buddhist cultural center in New York City in the waning moments of the last millennium, how could I have known that our fast friendship would evolve into what is surely the most important creative collaboration of my artistic life thus far?

A discussion about art, music, theatre and the vicissitudes of our respective lives became a suite of songs on Nonesuch Records called *Phantom Moon*. During the making of that record Steven suggested I read the Ted Hughes translation of Frank Wedekind's *Spring Awakening* and that perhaps we could adapt it as a piece of musical theatre. My initial abrupt response was notoriously rude and disdainful—not of Steven's idea but the entire genre of musical theatre as a legitimately "cool" form of artistic expression. Though I now look back on my rock elitism as embarrassingly naive it certainly suited the anti-establishment energy needed to match Wedekind's own scathing attitude towards the institutions of his milieu—and so it turned out all right.

As I embark on recording new pieces of underscore for the latest production of the show at the Almeida I can only marvel at how fortunate I've been to be part of the life of the ever-changing and always-impactful work that is *Spring Awakening*.

JONATHAN GROFF & LEA MICHELE (*Melchior and Wendla, original New York production, 2006–8*)

This book you are holding in your hands is more than just another musical. The dialogue and lyrics in this script can transport and transform you. Most importantly, the words in this show were written for you.

We started our run in *Spring Awakening* together at the Atlantic Theater on May 19th, 2006 and finished our run on Broadway on May 18th, 2008. Those two years changed us forever. The show launched our careers, but more importantly it gave us a way to express ourselves during the most evolutionary time in our lives. The words and music created a catharsis that is still healing and moving every time we revisit this material.

In writing this show, Steven and Duncan have given a gift to every young generation of theater actors. The poetry in this writing is a vessel for endless self-expression.

Take these words and make them your own. We can't wait to watch you.

———

ANEURIN BARNARD (*Melchior, original London production, 2009*)

Spring Awakening means so much to me, as it really was the springboard to launching my acting career. I fought so hard to play Melchior, and every night I loved going on stage playing him as if every night was my last chance to do so! It gave me an opportunity to stretch my skills and bring to life an amazing character with huge depth for an actor to indulge in. The play and music will forever resonate within my soul.

EVELYN HOSKINS (*Thea, original London production, 2009*)

At twenty years old, when I was cast to play Thea in the original London production, I can remember saying that *Spring Awakening* was a musical for our generation. When I look back now, I realise it's a musical for every generation, something we can all relate to at whatever age. It reminds us of the pain, angst, longing, naivety, struggle, acceptance, anger and love of our journey from adolescence to adulthood. Which is exactly what we as a young cast were living through both on and off stage.

I remember feeling an awakening of identity whilst working on the show. We were all so young and still discovering ourselves as people and for the first time as professional actors. Since then we've been given the privilege of perspective, bringing with it new meaning to each lyric and chord, a new empathy to feel for these characters on stage that we can all relate to. An inclusiveness, no matter what nationality, race, gender, sexuality or religion, because puberty is something we all must go through. The interconnectivity of this play, the emotion that the music brings, is something we can all appreciate differently over time—and, I'm sure, for years to come.

IWAN RHEON (*Moritz, original London production, 2009*)

Spring Awakening was the beginning. The words, music and universal message changed my life forever, as it has for so many. I'm sure it will continue to do so because living can be a bit of a bitch.

=

RUPERT GOOLD (*director, London revival, 2021*)

In the autumn of 2007 I went to New York with my wife on a theatre recce. I had heard of the sensation that was *Spring Awakening* but our trip was brief and the only night we had free was the day we arrived, so we got off the plane, threw down our bags, and headed straight to the Eugene O'Neill Theatre. As we bundled in at what was gone 2 a.m. to our jet-lagged minds I realised that this was actually the first show I'd ever seen on Broadway. Was it always this buzzy and young? The lights went down and like an hallucinatory dream out stepped the imperious but seemingly infant Lea Michele. She hopped insouciantly onto a chair clad in a strange kindergarten dress and suddenly began to sing with an ache and intensity that I can still recall fourteen years later as though it was yesterday. My wife turned to me and muttered "What on earth is this?" This was *Spring Awakening*, a show I couldn't initially make out at all. Its music was intoxicating, its form chaotic, its lyrics opaque, its sentiment ambiguous, its youth electrifying. It was a show I couldn't decide if I adored or was baffled by, but like all great theatre experiences it burned itself into my memory and I've returned to it every year since. I still don't entirely understand it. I still have all the feelings.

Spring Awakening is a famously unlikely source text for a Broadway musical with its scenes of suicide, masturbation and teenage pregnancy. Even more challenging than its content is its form, the scenes fragmented, expressionist shards of what Wedekind called a "children's tragedy." What Steven and Duncan have done so brilliantly is cleave to that fragmentary form but elegantly draw out a love story, a tragic friendship and above all a sense of deep comradeship between these disparate and dissolute teenagers. The story is broadly as Wedekind would recognise (with some clever extrapolations) but the songs are the cracks that let the light in. It's in these personal expressions of hope and vulnerability, closer to lyric poems than conventional Broadway "numbers," that the show finds its heart. The more austere or brutal the scene, the more glittering and heartfelt the songs in opposition. Some may find their opacity remote or confusing—but to me when someone asks "What exactly is a purple summer?", I say don't look for the answer in your mind but in your heart. If you give yourself to *Spring Awakening*, it will stay with you forever.

Steven Sater (book and lyrics) was awarded Tony Awards and Drama Desk Awards for Best Book and Best Score, the Grammy Award for Best Musical Show Album, as well as the Tony, Drama Desk, New York Drama Critics' Circle, Olivier, and Critics'  Circle Theatre Awards for Best New Musical for *Spring Awakening*. His other musicals with Duncan Sheik include *Alice by Heart* (National Theatre, MCC Theater); *The Nightingale* (La Jolla Playhouse); and *Nero* (Magic Theatre, NYSAF). Sater's musicals with other collaborators include *Prometheus Bound* (music by Serj Tankian, A.R.T.); *Some Lovers* (music by Burt Bacharach, The Old Globe, The Other Palace); and *Murder at the Gates* (music by James Bourne, The Other Palace, The Huntington Theatre). His plays include *Arms on Fire* (Steppenwolf New Play Prize, Chester Theatre Company); *New York Animals* (Bedlam); *Perfect for You, Doll* (Rosenthal Prize, Cincinnati Playhouse in the Park); and a reconceived musical version of Shakespeare's *Tempest* (Lyric Hammersmith). Additionally, Sater works as a poet, screenwriter and a pop lyricist. He has created television projects for HBO, Showtime, FX, NBC and Amazon, and his songs have been recorded by a host of popular musicians, from Michael Bublé to Leslie Odom Jr. His novel of *Alice by Heart* is published by Razorbill/Penguin Random House. The Grammy-nominated concept album of *Burt Bacharach and Steven Sater's Some Lovers* was released by Broadway Records in 2021.

NINA SUBIN

Duncan Sheik (music) launched his career in 1996 with his Grammy-nominated self-titled debut album. Sheik is the composer for the critically acclaimed musical *Spring Awakening*, which went on to win eight Tony Awards in 2007, including awards for

MYRNA SUAREZ

Best Orchestrations and Best Original Score. The album also earned Sheik a Grammy Award for Best Musical Show Album. In the years since, Sheik has released multiple albums, most recently *Legerdemain* in 2015 and *American Psycho: Original London Cast Recording*. The latter, with lyrics and music written by Sheik, premiered on Broadway in 2016 after a sold-out London run. He is currently working on a new album of original material as well as several theatre projects, including *Secret Life of Bees* (Atlantic Theater Company), *Alice by Heart* (MCC Theater), *Because of Winn Dixie* (Goodspeed) and *Lover, Beloved* (Alley Theatre).

Spring Awakening premiered on June 15, 2006 at the Atlantic Theater Company in New York City. This production transferred to Broadway, opening on December 10, 2006. In 2007, *Spring Awakening* was awarded the Tony Award for Best Musical (in addition to seven other Tony Awards, including Best Book and Best Original Score), The Dramatists Guild Hull-Warriner Award, the Lucille Lortel Award for Outstanding Musical, the Drama Desk Award for Outstanding Musical, the New York Drama Critics' Circle Award for Best Musical, the Drama League Award for Best Production of a Musical and the Outer Critics Circle Award for Best Musical. The original cast album was released by Decca in 2006. It opened in London at the Lyric Hammersmith on January 23, 2009, before transferring to the Novello Theatre in the West End on March 21, 2009. The production was awarded four Olivier Awards, including the prize for Best Musical.

ALMEIDA
THEATRE

The Almeida Theatre makes brave new work that asks big questions: of plays, of theatre and of the world around us.

Whether new work or reinvigorated classics, the Almeida brings together the most exciting artists to take risks; to provoke, inspire and surprise our audiences.

Recent highlights include *The Tragedy of Macbeth* (featuring Saoirse Ronan and James McArdle); Lolita Chakrabarti's *Hymn* (also broadcast on Sky Arts); Rupert Goold's productions of *Albion* (also broadcast on BBC Four) and his Olivier and Tony Award-winning production of *Ink* (also West End and Broadway); Rebecca Frecknall's Olivier Award-winning production of *Summer and Smoke* (also West End); and Robert Icke's productions of *Hamlet* (also West End and broadcast on BBC Two) and *The Doctor* (due to transfer to the West End in 2022).

Saoirse Ronan (Lady Macbeth) and James McArdle (Macbeth) in *The Tragedy of Macbeth* by William Shakespeare, directed by Yaël Farber at the Almeida Theatre (2021). Photo by Marc Brenner.

almeida.co.uk

Artistic Director **Rupert Goold**

Executive Director **Denise Wood**

Associate Director **Rebecca Frecknall**

🐦 @AlmeidaTheatre

👤 /almeidatheatre

📷 @almeida_theatre

Registered Charity no. 282167

Supported using public funding by
**ARTS COUNCIL
ENGLAND**

THE ASSASSINATION OF KATIE HOPKINS
Chris Bush and Matt Winkworth

ASSASSINS
Stephen Sondheim and John Weidman

THE BAND'S VISIT
David Yazbek and Itamar Moses

CAROLINE, OR CHANGE
Tony Kushner and Jeanine Tesori

COMPANY
1996 Broadway Production
and 2018 West End Revival
Stephen Sondheim and George Furth

CRUSH
Maureen Chadwick and Kath Gotts

DEAR EVAN HANSEN
Steven Levenson, Benj Pasek and Justin Paul

FOLLIES
Stephen Sondheim and James Goldman

A FUNNY THING HAPPENED
ON THE WAY TO THE FORUM
Stephen Sondheim, Burt Shevelove and Larry Gelbart

GIRL FROM THE NORTH COUNTRY
Bob Dylan and Conor McPherson

GYPSY
Stephen Sondheim, Arthur Laurents and Jule Styne

IMPROBABLE FREQUENCY
Arthur Riordan

INTO THE WOODS
1987 Broadway Production
and 2014 Film Tie-in Edition
Stephen Sondheim and James Lapine

LAZARUS
David Bowie and Enda Walsh

THE LIGHT IN THE PIAZZA
Craig Lucas and Adam Guettel

A LITTLE NIGHT MUSIC
Stephen Sondheim and Hugh Wheeler

LONDON ROAD
Alecky Blythe and Adam Cork

MISS YOU LIKE HELL
Quiara Alegría Hudes and Erin McKeown

THE NEW AMERICAN MUSICAL
Edited by Wiley Hausam
RENT — *Jonathan Larson*
FLOYD COLLINS — *Tina Landau and Adam Guettel*
THE WILD PARTY — *Michael John LaChiusa and George C. Wolfe*
PARADE — *Alfred Uhry and Jason Robert Brown*

NEXT TO NORMAL
Brian Yorkey and Tom Kitt

ONCE
Enda Walsh, Glen Hansard and Markéta Irglová

PACIFIC OVERTURES
Stephen Sondheim and John Weidman

PASSION
Stephen Sondheim and James Lapine

ROAD SHOW
Stephen Sondheim and John Weidman

THE SECRET GARDEN
Marsha Norman and Lucy Simon

A STRANGE LOOP
Michael R. Jackson

SUNDAY IN THE PARK WITH GEORGE
Stephen Sondheim and James Lapine

SWEENEY TODD
Stephen Sondheim and Hugh Wheeler

URINETOWN
Greg Kotis and Mark Hollmann